Missionary, Come Back!

by Arden Almquist

Missionary,
Come Back!

The World Publishing Company

NEW YORK AND CLEVELAND

Published by The World Publishing Company
2231 West 110th Street, Cleveland, Ohio 44102
Published simultaneously in Canada by
Nelson, Foster & Scott Ltd.

First Printing—1970

Library of Congress Catalog Card Number: 75-106069
Printed in the United States of America

WORLD PUBLISHING
TIMES MIRROR

ACKNOWLEDGMENTS

Acknowledgment is gratefully made to the following for permission to
quote from the sources indicated.

ABINGDON PRESS
From "Missionary Imperatives: A Conservative and Evangelical Exposition," by Harold Lindsell, and also from "Toward a Reformation of
Objectives" by Richard Schaull, both in *Protestant Crosscurrents in Mission*, ed. Norman A. Horner. Copyright 1968.

THE CHRISTIAN CENTURY
From "The American Missionary Problem" by Frederick Dale Bruner.
Copyright 1968 by the Christian Century Foundation.

COVENANT PRESS
From "Paul Carlson, Martyr" by Arden Almquist in *There Was a Man*,
ed. Carl Philip Anderson. Copyright 1965.
From *Salvation and Secularity* by Wesley W. Nelson. Copyright 1969.

DIVISION OF CHRISTIAN EDUCATION,
From *The Revised Standard Version of the Bible*. Copyright 1946 and
1952 by the Division of Christian Education, National Council of the
Churches of Christ in the U.S.A.

DOUBLEDAY & COMPANY, INC.
From *The Lonely African* by Colin M. Turnbull (Anchor Books Edition).
Copyright 1963.

FORTRESS PRESS

From *The Primal Vision* by John V. Taylor. Copyright 1963. Reprinted by permission of Fortress Press and S.C.M. Press, Ltd.

JOHN KNOX PRESS

From *Trinitarian Faith and Today's Mission* by Lesslie Newbigin. Copyright 1964. Reprinted by permission of John Knox Press and Edinburgh House Press.

FREDERICK A. PRAEGER, INC.

From *Burden of Empire* (Hoover Institution Publications) by L. H. Gann and Peter Duignan. Copyright 1967. Reprinted by permission of Frederick A. Praeger, Inc., and Pall Mall Press, Ltd.

THE MACMILLAN COMPANY

From *The New Testament in Modern English* translated by J. B. Phillips. Used by permission of the Macmillan Company and Geoffrey Bles, Ltd.

MARYKNOLL PUBLICATIONS

From "Collegiality, Mission, and Laity," by Thomas E. Clarke, and from "Individual Group Responsibility for the Needy Churches," by John A. Bell in *Revolution in Missionary Thinking*, ed. William J. Richardson. Copyright 1966.

WILLIAM MORROW & COMPANY, INC.

From *The Dark Eye in Africa* by Laurens van der Post. Copyright 1955. Used by permission of William Morrow & Company and the Hogarth Press, Ltd.

THE WESTMINSTER PRESS

From *World Cultures and World Religions* by Hendrik Kraemer. Copyright 1960, Hendrik Kraemer. Used by permission of The Westminster Press and the Lutterworth Press, London.

TO MY FATHER
WHO GAVE ME MY FIRST
UNDERSTANDING OF MISSION

Contents

Foreword

Most of today's books on mission and the missionary are too dated to inform us, or too dull to stir us, or too distorted to guide us.

This book has none of these black marks on it. On the contrary, I have found it to be an exceptionally rewarding and stimulating piece of work. Let me say four things about it:

(1) No reader will fail to be impressed by the author's desire to take the kinks out of the imbalances in our current missionary thinking and to restore to us both the length and the breadth of the perspective we need. Negatively put, Dr. Almquist's thesis is that the day of the "foreign missionary"—the witness who crosses cultural and religious frontiers—is *not* past. Positively stated, it is that missionaries are still needed, still have immensely meaningful opportunities, and that this will continue to be true. The author's handling of the thesis shows how well he has maintained equilibrium amid the swirling currents of circumstance and emotion by which a lot of us have been swept off our feet. The book's title, for example—*Missionary, Come Back!*—does not really surface until the reader has been exposed to a whole range of facts and reasons that lie behind the more familiar cry of recent years, "Missionary, go home!"

A quite different sort of redress for imbalances will be found in the author's second look at colonialism (including the Belgian form of it in Congo) and the offering of evidence to show that it was not *all* bad. Or, in a still different area of concern, I think of the corrective we now need for a lot of recent attempts to debunk and "de-halo" the missionary and his character. It is a process, to be sure, in which missionaries themselves have participated, from motives not always easy to isolate. Get them off their pedestal. They are, after all, such human, fallible, ordinary mortals! So we have been told repeatedly. Almost overdue, therefore, are Dr. Almquist's words about the missionary presence as a kind of conscience-presence: "and to be a conscience requires an exemplary life, free from impurity or disharmony in one's family relationships, or carelessness or corruption in finances, wherever one touches them, or covetousness about things or power, or coldness in communication." And he adds: "Faulty, yes. Imperfect, yes. Nevertheless, worthy of being followed."

(2) In an authentic and inoffensive way, these chapters will tell you much about the author. As certainly as there is an indecent, there is also a decent self-exposure, a healthy way of being confessional without being exhibitionist. You will find that here. The author is no detached reporter. He has been through the fire, and the singeing marks of it are on him. I believe it was Ralph Waldo Emerson who, when asked what he had thought of a sermon, replied, "It was not a bad sermon, but the preacher made me feel that he had never experienced either great joy or great sorrow." No fear of that here! Each chapter bears witness to the author's concern and dedication to the missionary task.

(3) The book is marked by the author's concern for precision in the language he uses and the explanations he gives. Even an attempt to be precise is more than we get in most quarters today. Goodman Ace recently began his *Saturday Review* col-

umn with the tart observation: "A new four-letter word has insidiously crept into our daily dialogue. The word is 'They.' As in: '*They* are all alike. *They* don't want to work.'" With those simple declarative sentences, containing that sweepingly nebulous pronoun, the speaker fancies he has blown to bits the whole movement for civil rights and poverty reform. In contrast, Dr. Almquist takes the phrase "younger churches," used frequently in the literature of missions, and devotes a seven-line footnote to his attempt to take the ambiguity out of it.

(4) Furthermore, I would commend these chapters for the fresh insights they uncover. What is the relationship between our American popularity obsession and our supersensitiveness to criticism? What is the connection between American affluence and missionary softness? What is the singular significance of "presence" in many African cultures? What is the contemporary form that may be taken by New Testament apostolic authority? What can a Western physician learn about psychosomatic illnesses by practicing sensitively in Africa? In what ways is it possible for today's missions to become innovative without sacrifice of their essential witness? If the identification principle is important to missionary witness and influence, what is at the core of the principle? Is it possible for religious jargon to reinforce, rather than remove, the mask that the missionary wears while attempting to reach nationals with the gospel?

All I can say is that if you want to be pricked and probed on any of these points, you will do well to take these chapters seriously. Even in places where you want to argue with the author, as I did when it came to his easy acceptance of Zabriskie's faulty exegesis of Acts 10:9–16, in Chapter 7, you will find illumination in the practical point that is being driven home.

In sum, this is a wise, realistic, and encouraging book—worth anybody's time to read.

—PAUL S. REES

Author's Introduction

Numerous voices have declared that the era of overseas mission is finished for Western Christendom. The cry of the new nations in this post-colonial era, we are told, is "Missionary, Go Home!" That there is legitimacy in the claim and justification for the cry cannot be denied. But it reflects only part of the picture and as such is a half-truth, with all the inherent dangers of half-truths. Thus, for example, its effect on a church seeking to remain faithful to the Great Commission in a world with more people to be won for Christ than ever before, as well as on missionaries themselves, is at the least disconcerting, and at the worst disastrous.

I am convinced that the era of intercontinental mission has just begun, that God has not rescinded the missionary mandate, and that a significant segment of those nations which have been exposed to foreign missionaries is on the contrary saying, "Missionary, Come Back!"

That conviction is derived from extensive travel and observations in Asia, Africa, and Latin America, as well as throughout our own country and Europe, and after numerous conversations with both missionaries and nationals of many lands, not all of them churchmen. What I thought I saw, and heard them say, I felt to be corroborated by a recent personal re-immersion for most of a year in overseas mission (after five years as a mission administrator) in an area where I earlier spent ten years as a medical missionary, namely, the Democratic Republic of the Congo.

This book therefore is a kind of personal testament of what one missionary in constant dialogue with the world and the church at home and abroad believes about his and his colleagues' role in a changing yet unchanged world—unchanged, that is, in its need of Christ as Lord and Savior. It is also an *apologia* for mission by one committed to the Great Commission, to the Uniqueness of Him who gave it, and to its continued, indeed, increasing relevance in an apocalyptic age. To a church newly awakened to long neglected domestic responsibilities, it is a plea not to redress one wrong by committing another, for the answer to the problems of the minorities at home is *not* the abandonment of the majorities abroad, for their needs are essentially the same, and the solutions to their problems inseparable.

This book is written for people who like to look at both sides of a subject; for students young and old, as well as their teachers; for laymen and ministers alike concerned for the relevance of the church; and, of course, for missionaries and those who serve on the boards and staffs that send them.

It is divided into four parts. Part I, entitled "Missionary, Go Home!," takes cognizance of the familiar post-colonial cry, affirming its validity in three chapters, the first through personal reminiscence: "Congo Revisited"; the second through historical review: "A Legacy of Barriers"; and the third through a look at the present-day evidence: "Is the Cry Contemporary?"

Part II, entitled "Missionary, Come Back!," attempts to make an objective appraisal of the opposite point from three different approaches: First, Chapter 4, "The Other Side of

the Coin," concludes from personal experience and current reporting in church journals that there *is* another side to the question of continued missionary presence. Chapter 5, "The Other
Legacy," takes a second look at the colonial era and finds it
wasn't all bad. Chapter 6, "The Recovery of Sent-ness," re-
examines the question of the missionary mandate and the sense of
call.

Having concluded that the plea "Missionary, Come Back!"
is legitimate and deserving of an affirmative response we seek to
suggest "The Way Back" in Part III. First, we must "Accept
The World" (Chapter 7), as a proper response both to God's
Word and to modern secularization. Secondly, we should "Pitch
A Tent" (Chapter 8), accepting the widespread movement of
Christian laymen abroad as a twentieth-century diaspora no less
significant for witnessing to our world on behalf of Christ than
was the first-century diaspora for early Christians. Thirdly, we
must become "All Things to All Men" (Chapter 9), in the full
Pauline sense, finding and employing those techniques which will
"by all means save some" (I Cor. 9:22 KJV).

Finally, in Part IV, we echo the African plea "Come, and
Lay Your Bones." Chapter 10, entitled "Career Mission—A
Live Option?," reaffirms the continued relevance of the career
missionary. Chapter 11 examines "Mission as Presence." And
in a concluding chapter we discuss "Mission as Cross," choosing
to illustrate the issue of missionary identification with the people
served by reference to Dr. Paul Carlson. (In this choice I do
not claim objectivity. Dr. Carlson was a personal friend, and like
myself, a physician and Covenanter).

My chief aim is to redress a felt imbalance and make the
point "Missionary, Come Back!" I have not attempted to define
a theology of mission and have left undiscussed many issues
which the reader may feel should have been included in a volume on mission. I do not, for example, treat any of the current

polarities in mission in any depth: the ecumenical-evangelical encounter, the tension between service and evangelism, or between
institutional and apostolic mission. I give only brief attention to
the church growth thesis, and less to the new technological aids
in communication. All of these subjects I feel are adequately cov-
ered by other writers.

My thanks are due to my wife Jo Ann, who has shared a
rather hectic life with me both at home and abroad, and willingly
surrendered vacation time to see this volume come to print; to my
typist, Miss Nancy Peckenpaugh, and particularly to my secretary,
Miss Arlene Norman, without whose help a finished manuscript
would not have been possible; and to a host of missionary and
national friends who were my inspiration.

I also wish to thank Carl Philip Anderson of Covenant
Press, Chicago, for repeated encouragements to write, as well as
for permission to use "Reflections on a Legacy," *Covenant Quarterly*, February 1964; and the Missionary Research Library
(New York), *Occasional Bulletin*, April 1967, for permission to
use "Medicine and Religion—A Missionary Perspective."

Part 1

Missionary, Go Home!

Chapter 1

CONGO REVISITED

"Keep a diary your first year," one mission executive quietly suggests to freshmen missionaries going overseas for their first term. "Your first impressions are probably the right ones! And make it a point," he continues after a pause, "to reread it on each anniversary of your arrival in the field. You may be surprised at what you wrote, and wonder what has happened to you since you wrote it."

That was not the usual advice given to new missionaries when I went overseas the first time in the summer of 1951. It was rather more customary to compliment the novice for his enthusiasm, and then softly caution him to keep quiet his first term and learn from the older missionaries.

Thus it was with no small pain and effort that I sat down in an overstuffed swivel chair behind a large mahogany desk in Chicago after more than a decade in the Congo bush to assume the role of a mission executive, and, with no personal diary before me, tried to recall the initial impressions I had had as a young missionary.

I was at once surprised to sense how right those early impressions seemed from this new perspective. Indeed, the material that emerged from that deliberate reverie seems now, in further retrospect, most suggestive of the reasons why the cry "Missionary, Go Home!" came to be uttered. And while our concern is to make the counter point "Missionary, Come Back!" it may serve us well to begin there.

I am going to try to recover the sense of shock which I felt as a missionary novice entering the then Belgian Congo for the first time in August 1952. The emergence of the Congo as an independent nation seemed rather remote then. That was more than thirty nations ago, among them the Democratic Republic of the Congo itself. The very fact that the independence of the Congo could have then seemed remote to most observers of the African scene is itself an indication of our need to see it once again through the eyes of an idealistic newcomer.

I shall do so by describing some typical scenes depicting white-black relations, some of them from the European community, others from the missionary community. I am convinced that a fundamental factor behind current missionary frustration is the problem of communication, and that the legacy from which we operate—a legacy in part revealed by the scenes we describe—is a significant element in our difficulty.

We arrived in Léopoldville, "Léo," as everyone called it then, which occupied in part the old city of Kinshasa, as it is now called. (The renaming of the capital is itself highly suggestive!) Focus of the once thriving Bakongo empire, whose territory had long been straddled by the colonies of three European states—Portugal, France, and Belgium—it is a fabulous city with towering buildings, broad streets, and modern stores full of goods, throbbing with activity; it seemed to reflect a prodigious effort to combine Old World beauty with New World pragmatism in an African setting. But I was struck at once by the sharp contrast between the splendor of the European sector—greater than that known by most Belgians in Brussels or Antwerp—and the relative squalor of the African sector. True, there were no separate fountains marked *blanc* and *noir* (Europeans don't drink water!). But in the stores and at the post office the whites were served first and the Africans made to wait. I was personally embarrassed when, taking my place at the end of a line at a postal window to buy stamps, I was summoned to the front by the African clerk at the window, ahead of four or five Congolese who preceded me. I searched their faces, expecting hostility, but they seemed almost relieved when I moved to the window.

We boarded the *Reine Astrid*—a stern-wheeling river boat that looked like it had just churned its way out of the pages of a Mark Twain Mississippi novel—for our week-long trip up country on the Congo River. It was a memorable voyage, a leisurely introduction to the tropical wonderland that was to be our home. Vachel Lindsay penned his reaction to a first view of the river in the words:

> Then I saw the Congo, creeping through the black,
> Cutting through the jungle with a golden track.[1]*

It is a wide river, the third largest in the world, unbridged from Kisangani (formerly Stanleyville) to the mouth, tawny yellow in hue, a protoplasmic ribbon living in a kind of symbiosis with the encroaching forest, dotted with islands large and small, like so many inclusion bodies engulfed through the membranous shoreline. Here and there appeared a lone fisherman's hut, and once I saw a deserted village, a deathly silent witness to the terror that is the trypanosome, the parasite that causes sleeping sickness.

Our European staterooms were ample, and though the ship was a bit crowded, meals were provided, there was space for lounging on the deck, and we had some facilities for entertainment. True, it was noisy. The *Reine Astrid* was a wood-burning

---

* Notes follow final chapter; see p. 193.

vessel, and we stopped every night to take on the next day's fuel
supply. The loading filled most of the hours of the night, and
the clatter of logs mingled with the rhythmic singing of the black
porters.

The African passengers were crowded below in miserably
small rooms with no meal service. Each brought along such food
as he could, supplementing along the way by buying from the
vendors who lined the shore at every port. Stops were infre-
quent—about one a day—but occasionally an enterprising sales-
man would attach his dugout canoe to the moving ship and sell
his smoked fish and *kwanga* (a kind of native bread) and grubs
to the passengers lined up on the lower deck. It was risky business, requiring a deft and perfectly timed maneuver. Once a
pirogue capsized, and the hapless merchant could be seen swim-
ming downstream trying to catch his canoe as our boat pulled
out of range. No effort was made to help him by the European
crew, and the Africans below greeted the catastrophe with
peals of laughter.

Upon arrival up-country we stopped at the local territorial
office to be inscribed on the register. The African policeman in
faded blue uniform saluted us sharply (if a bit ludicrously)
as we mounted the crumbling concrete stairs of the thick-walled,
veranda-circled, high-ceilinged, thatch-roofed building. A score
of Africans dressed for the most part in ill-fitting cast-off pieces
of Western clothing came to attention of a sort, and those sitting
or lolling on the porch rose to their feet. The missionary who
accompanied us introduced us to the Belgian clerk, seated just
inside the common hall of the several offices, who stood and extended his hand warmly, and then introduced us in turn to the
other three members of the territorial staff—the white members, that is. There were African assistants in each of the various
offices as well as white officials, but no one bothered to introduce us to them. When I offered a handshake to one whom I
met just inside the doorway, he seemed embarrassed. The Afri-

cans were addressed by first name only—Pierre, or Jean, or simply *boi*, never as *monsieur*, and the Belgians used the familiar form of address in speaking to them, *tu* instead of *vous*, as a man would address his child—or his dog.

It was scarcely different when we arrived at the mission station that evening. Under missionary supervision the Africans helped unload the truck and carry in our paraphernalia. Then they made for the native village to find food and lodging for the night. The whites sat down to eat as a missionary group, alone except for the forty- to fifty-year-old "boy" who served our table, very black in his white T-shirt and shorts, summoned for his services by a little bronze bell in reach of the hostess' hand.

One evening after we were settled, the local Belgian administrator invited us to be dinner guests in his home. The evening moved pleasantly. We had visited much of Belgium and conversation was easy. My wife chatted with *madame* and I with *monsieur*. Two mulatto children, products of his earlier term as a bachelor, sat stiffly silent, until their white stepmother's sharp command sent them to bed. In the course of the evening's conversations we were offered advice on white-black relations:

"These people are all children: Treat them as such and you'll get along."

"You can't joke with these people. Africans have no sense of humor."

"Never trust your domestics. They'll steal you blind."

"Never make an adverse comment about another European in the hearing of Africans."

"Always preserve your dignity."

Later I was to visit a dispensary on the Uele River at the village of Ndolanga. It was a large village of nearly two thousand people accessible only by pirogue, and ruled by old chief Ngbo, who had thirty wives. A throng of children crowded around me, many of them bearing his features, eager to see the new *monganga* (doctor), matched in their curiosity and noisy jubilation by their adult peers. In a moment of exuberance inspired by their ingenuousness and spontaneity, I picked up a chair and balanced it on my chin, juggled some oranges, skinned the cat on a tree branch, and hung from the branch by my toes. They were utterly delighted and howled with glee, and from that moment on I belonged to that village.

Some weeks later we had coffee with the local sanitary agent at his home. An African clerk appeared for a moment to ask me about his wife, who was a patient in our hospital at Wasolo. I had come to admire him as a person of unusual talent and promise. He had left a Catholic seminary to enter state service, and we had discussed theology and philosophy together in my home on his occasional visits to the mission. The Belgian gave him leave to talk with me briefly, but he did not offer him a chair, nor invite him to join us in a cup of coffee. The African showed no sign of being offended, and spoke with utmost graciousness. When he left, I commented on his remarkable qualities. The white man agreed, remarked about his intelligence and trustworthiness, and then added wistfully, "I wish we had more men like him—he's almost white." And then, "But you know—I wouldn't think of asking Andrew into my home!"

I understood the foreboding in Joseph Conrad's magnificent *Heart of Darkness* a bit better after that experience, and after another which occurred a few days later. A local African chief of athletic build and easy manner called on me at our house in the late afternoon. At his appearance we both put out our hands and shook warmly, snapping our fingers at the moment of separating the grip in the manner of the Ngbandi. He looked at me squarely, then spoke: "That's what's different about you missionaries. You shake hands with us."

What a simple thing, a handshake—and how profound! By it the white man in Africa classed himself, for many did *not* shake hands with Africans. In this the Belgians were like the South Africans, and like them, only sooner, they would write their own epitaph with their own unshaken, unsoiled, and un-shared hand.

But though the missionary shook hands with the African, instinctively aware that he shared with him a common humanity, ignoring for Christ's sake the threat of disease real or imagined offered by the outstretched, fingerless, and ulcerated hand of the victim of leprosy, for example, as a white man he was not free from the impediments of his race and culture.

I was visiting a busy missionary in his office one forenoon early in my period of Lingala language study. It was a small room, rather dark in spite of copious whitewash, with no windows except for two screens provided with rough wooden shutters that were raised and hooked to a pole supporting the overhanging grass roof to admit light and air. One of the screens had a curious little door in the lower left-hand corner, near the missionary's desk and in reach of his left arm. It reminded me of the little door within a door that dog- and cat-lovers in the States sometimes had for the ingress and egress of their pets. I had noticed one in every missionary's office. Pointing with a nod, I asked the missionary about it.

"What's the little window for?"

"Oh that. For convenience, I guess. It's just a handy way to see people."

"Couldn't they use the door?"

"Oh, there're too many coming all the time. It's less of an interruption this way. I've never really given it a thought. We've always done it this way."

"But I've never seen white people come to the window. They always use the regular door."

There was a pause, and a hint of a flush on his tanned face. He leaned back in his chair and spoke slowly, his gaze directed at a point beyond and over my own, in the manner of a professor unsure of his subject and unwilling to meet his pupil's gaze.

"That's different. After all, there are very few whites here, and there's a—well, a kind of bond between us, you know. You can't expect a white man to stand outside when he comes. You just naturally invite him in. With the Africans it's different. They don't expect to be asked into your office. The Belgians and Portuguese all follow this practice, and there's no reason for us to do differently."

He paused again, this time at some length. Suddenly he leaned forward and met my gaze with some earnestness.

"Look, I'll be frank with you. For one thing, there are just too many of them—Africans, I mean. Really, you wouldn't have any peace at all if you started letting them walk into your office. It saves a lot of time this way. We're all pretty busy doing the Lord's work, you know. Take paying the workers for just one example. Why, it'd take all day if they came into my office one by one! This way I can finish in an hour and a half. Besides, if I may say it, I like to keep my office clean. It rains a lot in this country, and I can't see letting every Tom, Dick, and Harry drag mud in here!"

His voice had become a bit animated as he developed his argument. We were interrupted by the appearance of a yard boy at the window with a note. Thanking the African, the missionary reached through the little window-door with his left hand. He excused himself to read the note, then turned to me again.

"It's a notice about missionary prayer meeting tonight. I rather enjoy it. It's one time one can be alone with his own comrades and pray in his own language. You're coming, of course?"

I nodded assent, excused myself for having imposed on his

time, and thanked him. He rose from his chair, put a hand on my shoulder and chuckled.

"You'll have a little window yourself before long, and wonder how it could ever have struck you as peculiar!"

As with the missionary's office, so was it also with his truck. Mission vehicles were white, whether the coat of paint they wore happened to be red or green or black. That became clear on my very first journey. I had wondered about it when the mission truck with a missionary driver met me at the river port as I got off the *Reine Astrid*. On that occasion I assumed that I rode up front and the Africans behind because I was being received as a guest. This time we were going to a missionary committee meeting. The three missionaries rode up front in the cab of the truck, and the African passengers in the rear. Among them were an evangelist on his way to a preaching mission in the bush; a nurse returning to the rural dispensary in his charge after a visit to the mission to get supplies; and an elderly chief going back to his village after a recent hernia operation. The rest of the passengers were a motley assortment of people who had sought rides and managed to wear our resistance down to the point of acquiescence. They sat on the trunks and boxes and drums that held our food and clothing and bedding and gasoline. It was the dry season, and the road was hot and dusty, although relatively smooth. During the rainy season, the passengers in the back would bounce constantly as the wheels struck the deep ruts and potholes in the road; or a rain squall would appear, and they would hover under a steamy-hot and flapping tarpaulin, commonly full of leaks.

We stopped for a bit of lunch along the way. The missionaries took out their thermoses and lunches of sandwiches, cold chicken, and bananas, and ate together, first asking God to bless the meal, while the Africans—if they had brought anything—

sauntered down the road a piece to unroll the leaves from their *kwanga* or nibble at a banana.

Eating was largely a segregated function, except on rare occasions. Not only was it unusual for an African to be seated at a white man's table; white men, including missionaries, rarely ate at an African's. I was giving the grand tour of the Wasolo mission one day to a visiting Norwegian missionary. It was mid-afternoon, and the mission workmen were seated outside their huts after having their daily bath following the cessation of the day's work. They were drinking coffee as we walked by and offered my guest and me a cup. I accepted mine, served in a glass, very black, and almost syrupy from too much sugar. My friend refused with a *"Non, merci!,"* then turned to me, saying in English: "Surely you don't drink with these people? Aren't you concerned about getting dysentery?"

But it was not only fear that handicapped the missionary. There was a kind of conspiracy of solidarity of race and culture that made him insensitive to his own basic humanity.

Christmas was an example. For weeks before and after Christmas the large SoTransCongo truck which tripled as commercial carrier, local bus, and mail wagon made its weekly stop at the Karawa post, disgorging each time a dozen sacks of mail, filled with parcels from the States—gifts for the missionaries and their "benighted" children whom the thoughtful donors imagined to be so exposed to the hazards of jungle life, and so cheated of the gimmicks of an ever-expanding affluent American society. For the African "boy" or nurse or teacher or pastor there were no gifts—they had no relatives overseas. There was tacit agreement among the missionaries—indeed at one time a station council ruling—that no individual missionary was to give a Christmas present to an African individual. Instead there was a Christmas party by the missionaries as a group for the Africans as a group.

This conspiracy of solidarity included the non-missionary members of the white race, the Belgians, Portuguese, and Greeks who made up the white community. Whatever their personal qualities or qualifications, or lack of them, they were recognized as "belonging" in a special way, although many of them showed little or no evidence of faith in Christ. Gradually, as the days became months, and the months years, one got caught up in these attitudes.

It was mid-morning at our busy Wasolo hospital. A Portuguese trader arrived at the mission with an aching tooth. I was expected to leave the Africans waiting at the hospital and tend to him. Having just had an operation on my hand and not yet having recovered the strength of my grip I took the precaution in my naïveté to ask the African nurse who was my right-hand man to come along and stand by in case I needed help. After several futile attempts to dislodge the tooth I turned to Nutombo and said: "Here, you try!" He hesitated a moment—long schooled in the ways of the Portuguese—but accepted the instrument. The white man closed his jaw firmly, shook his head "No!" and said: "Not *him*. NEVER. *You* do it!" With the blood hot in my ears, I acquiesced, and in the strength of my anger, yanked out the tooth.

There was a conspiracy of solidarity in the African community too, as rigid as our own, as an experience toward the close of my first term of four years made clear.

We had a strike at the Wasolo station. It began when I dismissed five student nurses. Quickly the solidarity of the African community manifested itself. The workmen quit working, and all building ceased. The schoolteachers sent the two hundred pupils home. Work at the hospital came to a standstill. It was my fault—I had injured the African's keen sense of justice in a burst of anger. It was easy to rationalize my deed. Four of the five had stolen medications, or accepted bribes for services, or been delinquent on duty. I had warned them, but to no avail. In exasperation I had summarily dismissed the class and told them to return to their villages. But I had done so in anger, and I had been unfair to one among the five whom everyone felt to be innocent. I talked it over with the senior missionary on the station, who smiled awkwardly and told me: "It's your problem. You got yourself into it. You'll have to handle it."

I returned to my room to pray together with my wife. Then, humbled, I took a can of powdered coffee and some sacks of sugar and went down to the African village where the strikers, in a sullen mood, were sitting around their small fires in front of their huts. I told them I was sorry, and asked them to forgive me. Then I invited them to add hot water from their cooking pots to the symbols of reconciliation in my hands, so that we might share a cup of coffee together and talk things over. They listened in silence, with growing interest. There were murmurs of surprise, and suddenly there was joy! We shook hands all around, and drank together. I agreed to review my hasty decision, and they agreed to return to work and recall the schoolchildren to their classes. There were tears and laughter, and someone said: "Doctor, this is the first time a white man ever apologized to us."

I walked back up to my hilltop house, filled with the joy of reconciliation. A myriad of goose pimples erupted on my skin—a fleshly microcosm of the familiar savannah, its surface dotted with anthills.

What a wonderful thing forgiveness! Every dry season vast sheets of flame whipped across the savannah, burning everything in their path, searing mercilessly the scraggly trees, and driving the hapless animals before them to seek shelter in the forest, the edges of which the fire gnawed, only to surrender to its eternal greenness and die there. And in two weeks' time the tender new grass sprang up, and the driven animals, whatever rancor they may have held against the Creator for this perilous interruption of their creature-life gone, filtered back into the newborn fields, grateful for the way of things . . . And the giant forest, too scarred for a few years to yield a garden, would reclaim the soil to enrich it again with its leaves that another generation of men might eat and live . . . And a patient would be brought to me horribly mauled by a leopard or a croc or a hippo or a pig or an elephant or a buffalo, and I would cut away the mangled flesh and the body of the man would say *"Likambo te, c'est la vie"* (Oh well, that's life)—and accept the mercies of God and penicillin and before long there was a man again, a whole creature.

John Taylor's recall of those fine lines from Middleton Murray's commentary on Keats's letters—so essentially African and so universal—aptly describes my mood:

> For this . . . kind of . . . forgiveness, which forgives not only man, but life itself, not the pains which men inflict but the pains which are knit up with the very nature of existence, we have no word. Let it be called . . . Acceptance.[2]

My dismissal of the nurses was not the only occasion on which I lost my temper. I include here a final vignette, because it is illustrative of the multitude of seemingly small daily incidents that scar the memories of countless unknown persons in Africa, Asia, and Latin America, impairing communication between the Western white man and the rest of the world.

It happened during my second term. My resources were at a low ebb, after a period of unusually exhausting circumstances. We were on a long journey and I was at the wheel of our Wasolo station one-and-a-half-ton Ford pickup truck. We were pushing hard over the dusty dry-season road and overtook an ancient rickety lorry pouring out clouds of black exhaust which mingled with the dust of the road raised by the two worn tires that graced the rear axle (made to carry four). We were in a hurry, and hated the dust and smoke and delay. I honked the horn for the road. The African chauffeur didn't yield and I leaned on the horn as I tailgated his truck with increasing exasperation. It all seemed a deliberate affront! After ten miles or so of this he pulled off on the side of the road to stop at a village. I drew alongside him, stopped, got out of my truck, walked over to him, and "ate him out," rejecting in no uncertain terms his simple insistence that he hadn't heard us. At the height of my lecture he reached into his shirt pocket, pulled out a worn and soiled card, and showed it to me. It read *Membre de l'Eglise du Christ au Congo* (Member of the Church of Christ of the Congo). That simple rebuke would live long in my memory. When I cooled down later it was to admit that he was doubtless speaking the truth, that he had indeed not heard me, and that I had been an ugly fool and a miserable witness to the saving grace of Christ, and *that* to a brother in the faith. But by then it was too late to apologize for my rudeness, and I never saw him again.

Perhaps it is better not to keep a diary after all! There is more than enough content in the events just recorded to suggest that.

The cry "Missionary, Go Home!" is obviously not without ground, even in the personal experience of the missionary sensitive to his role in the country to which his sense of call has led him. Not alone in Africa, but wherever history has written a chapter titled "The Colonialist Era," the missionary carries into his task what Elmer Neufeld calls a "Legacy of Barriers." It is only as we become aware of and understand this legacy that we can hope effectively to communicate with and witness to those on the other side of the barrier. For this legacy hinders every serious effort at honest communication between white and black, Westerner and non-Westerner, not only in Africa, but in all of Afericasia, as Donald McGavran likes to call collectively the nations of Africa, Latin America, and Asia—indeed, in our own United States as well.

Let us turn now to an examination in a less personal way of the content of this legacy.[3]

Chapter 2

A LEGACY OF BARRIERS

In an attempt to *feel* the background for the cry "Missionary, Go Home!" we have revisited the Congo through the medium of memory, and tried to recapture the original reactions of a young career missionary exposed for the first time to an actual field experience. Common to all the experiences thus relived is something that may be called "a legacy of barriers."

What is the content of this legacy? Beyond what is implied in the scenes depicted in Chapter One, scenes from my own experience and relatively recent, there is the *legacy of the distant past*, a memory affecting all white-black relations. It is the memory of the slave trade, that tragic era which sent 13,000,000 people out of the Congo alone in bonds![1] It is a memory etched in blood with chains and whips and long marches as beasts of burden; a memory of broken homes, of separation and sorrow, of thirst and hunger, of suffering, torture, and death. True, it was Africans themselves who sold other Africans into slavery, but it was largely the white man who created the market. True, the missionaries, with rare exceptions, did not themselves hold slaves, and it was mainly they who ultimately provided the conscience that stirred the events which led to the collapse of the practice. But for too long they acquiesced in the system, wittingly or unwittingly, and learned to live with it and its dehumanizing effects. Indeed, the earliest missions in Africa, such as those of the Capuchin monks of the seventeenth and eighteenth centuries, were frankly imperialistic, and the Africans they sought to reach were regarded as sub-human. Even if he were free of this history, today's white missionary shares in the legacy of the slave trade by the simple fact of being white, for at the time of that epoch all white men were automatically identified as Christians.

In the events of independence in 1960 and the rebellion of 1964 with the widespread evacuation of whites from the Congo which ensued we saw the fulfillment of the dictum given by our Lord: "Whoever exalts himself will be humbled" (Matt. 23:12 RSV).

I remember standing on the shore of the Ubangi River at the end of my second term in the Congo, caught up in the chaotic events of independence, watching a long pirogue with its precious cargo of missionary wives and children grow smaller and smaller and then disappear, as they evacuated the turbulent new land for the safety of the French territory on the other side. For a brief moment I wondered if I would ever see my wife and children again. The familiar Exodic scripture was strangely vivid and significant that day: "I the Lord thy God am a jealous God, visiting the iniquity of the fathers upon the children unto the third and fourth generation" (Exod. 20:5 RSV).

Truly the sin of the slave trade was visiting us that day! The 80,000 whites fleeing Congo at that moment were an exodus less than one one-hundred-fiftieth as great as that earlier and prolonged exodus which the evil slave trade had forced upon the Congo basin. How many families had been broken on the very shore where I stood? I at least hoped to see my wife and children again. *They* had separated—wife from husband, parent from child, brother from sister, lover from lover—knowing they would never see each other again! The long lines had marched sadly away, chained together, some sweating from the heavy burdens borne on their heads, others bleeding from the angry lashes of the whip, torn from home and kindred and the familiar presence of departed ancestors, to go they knew not where. They knew only that before them lay a long march, hunger, thirst, and torture, and a water so great a man's eye could not reach the distant shore, which they would cross in a monstrous boat, their bodies stacked like the wood a frugal wife hoarded when the rains began to fall; and for many of them, a cruel death.

I was a part of this legacy, there was no denying it, bearing in my own body the sins of my race.

Four years later we were to taste the cup of Africa's vengeance, when Dr. Paul Carlson, my successor at Wasolo, saw his wife and children safely evacuated at the same crossing as a result of the rebellion which swept the Congo, and returned to his patients only to be captured by the advancing rebel troops and die in Stanleyville during the rescue by Belgian paratroopers of the hundreds of white hostages held there by the *Simbas*, as the rebels were called.

Even with the passing of the slave trade—a victory largely produced by the early Protestant missionary movement which grew out of the spiritual revivals in the West and which nurtured a conscience that protested strongly against slavery—there followed another era in Leopold II's Congo whose memory still stalks the relations of whites and blacks. This was the era of free exploitation of the colonial peoples, marked by forced labor and production quotas, enforced by the whip and even by mutilation, the latter so fresh in the memory of the Congolese that when independence came, a few Belgians had their hands chopped off at the wrist—for some of Leopold's agents, as a means of stimulating rubber production, had resorted to the practice of severing one hand of men who failed to bring in their quota.

There is also the *legacy of the near past*, the still warm corpse of vanishing colonialism, the era of "the white man's burden," a time of mixed good and evil, blessing and curse, frankly espoused in the Congo as paternalism, in which many Belgian administrators honestly believed. *Dominer pour servir* was the motto, described in its classic form by Pierre Ryckmans,[2] and linked in its pursuit were the Belgian state, the Roman Catholic Church, and the mining, agricultural, industrial, and commercial companies. Under it the Africans' standard of living was improved, great strides were made in literacy and health, and much economic progress achieved.

Roads were built, crisscrossing even the remotest interior, tribal conflicts ended (for all time it was naïvely thought), and efficient administration introduced. Primary education expanded rapidly, and schools sprang up in the remotest villages. Sleeping sickness was virtually conquered, together with yaws and other diseases, while impressive medical centers sprang up throughout the land. Thousands of jobs were created, and a welfare society with universal care for every Congolese citizen from cradle to grave was emerging. Missions shared in the expanse, and numerous churches were built, some of them truly magnificent. But the Belgians learned in the Congo what the Dutch had learned with bitterness just a few years earlier in Indonesia—as so aptly described by Laurens van der Post:

> I shall never forget a sad, embittered moment after the war when the Dutch leaders in Java realized for the first time that the desire of the Indonesians to see them leave those lovely emerald islands of the East was no passing emotion and that their empire, the third largest in the world, was tumbling down about them. I remember the governor-general turning to me and saying, 'I cannot understand it. Look what we have done for them. Look at the schools and the hospitals we have given them. A hundred years ago

the population was only a few million, today it is nearly 60 million. We have done away with malaria, plague and dysentery and given them a prosperous, balanced economy. Everyone has enough to eat. We have given them an honest and efficient administration and abolished civil war and piracy. Look at the roads, the railways, the industries—and yet they want us to go. Can you tell me why they want us to go?' and I felt compelled to say, 'Yes, I think I can: I'm afraid it's because you've never had the right look in the eye when you spoke to them.'[3]

And under colonialism, a measure of forced labor remained, the whip was still used, although the number of stripes progressively diminished, and the cold prisons were kept full. The prisoners were a convenient work force, useful for working on roads and landscaping public grounds. Even the sick were a source of labor, for victims of sleeping sickness, yaws, and leprosy who failed to show up for their periodic injections under the efficient and regimented Belgian public health regime, and who lacked means to pay the fines imposed, would go to jail, and those among them not obviously incapacitated joined other law breakers in the work gangs. The black and yellow horizontally striped sweat shirts of the men and the similarly designed skirts of the women were a familiar sight, and except for this one difference in garb and the bare breasts of the women, there was little to distinguish the sexes, for the heads of the men and women were alike shorn, and they frequently worked together in the same crews.

No African élite was formed trained to lead a nation when independence should come, and the European and African communities were clearly separated with little communication between them. There were a few Belgians who deplored this state of affairs, but they were a small minority, and heard too late. There was no real equality, so that even the benefits began to appear as a trick for the continuation of the privileged status of the white man and the denial of the deeper aspirations of the black.

The missionary was not free from this legacy. His mission station reflected the European pattern all too closely, and the missions—whose voice and conscience had dealt the death blow to slavery—were generally caught up in the paternalistic mood. The system seemed almost right, because it accomplished much good. In exchange for the patronage of the state, the missions, almost without exception, acquiesced by silence in the inequalities and inherent wrongs of the colonial system. In accepting state subsidies for their schools and hospitals, they accepted Belgian paternalism, which consciously or unconsciously saw the African at best as a child.

From regarding Africans as children, it was not a long step to thinking of them as inferior, even when they became Christians. One felt the kind of shock I have tried to depict on arrival at obvious instances of brutality and the built-in inequalities, and gradually absorbed the pattern, however hard he may have tried to resist it by occasional gestures of defiance of European solidarity, or efforts at identification with the African community.

I remember well stopping at a village where a Belgian administrator was trying a group of men for an alleged crime, and chatting with him amiably for a few minutes before moving on. I was young and newly arrived, and missed the import of the gathering until the next day when one of the chiefs, Bangapa, came to me to be treated for several severe linear cuts on his buttocks. It was my introduction to the whip, the use of which had begun to be limited by the time of my arrival in the Congo in mid-1952 (the usual punishment had just been reduced from nine to four lashes), but which was still in use. Bangapa could hardly have failed to identify my conviviality with the Belgian administrator as tacit approval of what he was about to do.

Missionaries have been charged with helping to soften up

the colonial peoples for their take-over by European powers and the charge is not without some basis in fact. Rarely did they do so consciously. But the ties were close between colonial administrators and missionaries, who often indicated a preference for being together, and shared a measure of social life commonly denied to the people among whom they worked. Sharing a common culture, a common race, certain common privileges, and to a degree, a common power, it was natural that they should be lumped together in the mind of the national. Often these ties were further strengthened by common nationality.

The majority of missionaries in a given colonial or ex-colonial country tend to share the nationality of the European nation that has dominated their history. In the Belgian Congo the majority of missionaries were Belgian Roman Catholics, and consultation between the Governor General and the Archbishop was frequent, facilitated by the fact that their offices were adjacent. In 1925 a convention between the government and church placed all education of Congolese children in the hands of the Roman Catholic Church. Not until 1948 were Protestants included in the convention.[4] And only as late as 1955 were government lay schools established. In Mozambique and Angola the Roman Church remains in charge of education to this day.

When riots struck Kinshasa (then Léopoldville) in 1958, the mob attacked Catholic missions in the city, sparing Protestant centers in this initial assault. The Catholic missions, largely Belgian-run, were clearly associated with the colonial power in the Congolese mind, and suffered from the identification.

On March 20, 1968, I attended the dedication of the Paul Carlson Evangelical Medical Center in the Ubangi in the northern Congo. A group of ten Americans flew in for the event from the States, members of the foundation that established the center, as well as friends. The American Ambassador flew up from Kinshasa for the occasion to give a speech. One of the center's first projects was to host a research team from the Armed Forces Institute of Pathology in Washington, D.C. They brought in a great deal of laboratory and other equipment and were flown to Gemena, the nearest airport, in a large United States army plane, complete with camouflage. Congo-American relations were good at the moment, and the new medical center was founded as a non-mission project. But its staff were former missionaries, and there can be little doubt what associations were made in the minds of the local populace.

Indeed, some nationals feel strongly that missionaries are actual agents of the governments of the countries from which they come. I recall as a student in Brussels in 1951, learning French in what was then called the colonial course, sensing the suspicion toward me and my 150 American comrades in the course, that we were spies whose real aim under the guise of missionaries was to help prepare the United States to take over the Belgian colony. The increasing American presence in their former colony must have these same Belgians saying, "I told you so!"

Missions have in effect been administrative arms of the government under the Minister of Education. As "agents" of government they have had to be suppressive at times. When a revival broke out in the Ubangi in 1950 and some of the meetings in the churches became ecstatic and prolonged into the night, the missionaries of the Evangelical Mission of the Ubangi were told by the Belgian authorities to "cool it," and did. Not only was a spontaneous movement of the people suppressed—so was a probable work of the Holy Spirit!

Since the government of the Belgian Congo limited the training of Congolese to a certain level, missions accommodated themselves to that level. Perhaps they could not do otherwise. But it is little wonder that when independence caught the new Congo nation with too few leaders, the missionary force shared in the blame.

Certainly the missionary cannot free himself of the charge of having accepted privilege or even having cultivated it. Indeed an occasional missionary has unconsciously reveled in the superior position which the missionary situation gave him the opportunity to attain. In the competitive home situation he may actually have been a nobody. Lack of personnel has too often abetted this situation by throwing young missionaries into positions of leadership before they were sufficiently seasoned. And quite apart from rank and status, nearly all Western missionaries share in an abundance of possessions, including gadgetry, which, although less than what they might have enjoyed at home, nonetheless look like riches to the people among whom they live. Not the least of these riches is the opportunity afforded their children for a superior education in a segregated situation. Limited as the educational facilities for missionary children may be in contrast with the typical high school or private academy at home, to the African parent scrounging for money to buy a slate and a supply of chalk for a son attending a typical Congo bush school, these same facilities must look plush indeed.

The school for missionary children has not been the only segregated mission institution. The mission station in general has been a segregated place. Missionaries came by segregation naturally, of course. Most of them grew up in segregated churches in the homeland. Then, too, like all mortals they are subject to the invidious power of rationalization. They share the humanity of the rich young ruler, and like him, when Jesus confronts them, find it easy to justify themselves.

Segregation has tended further to be sustained by the subtle acceptance on the part of some missionaries of actual belief in the superiority of the white race. Once in a discussion of a particular disappointment involving an African nurse-aide with a missionary friend I was told quite candidly: "The trouble with you is that you really think these people are your equal. If you'd just accept the fact that the Negro is a member of an inferior race and plan your program accordingly, you'd have fewer problems."

A corollary of segregation has been the tendency for missionaries to withhold themselves from participation in local community life. The Congo, for example, celebrates many national holidays—too many to suit the average work-oriented missionary WASP who typifies the West. As a consequence many have made it a practice to stay away from such events, the while groaning about what's happening to the building or teaching or surgery in which they are engaged. Better that the missionary rejoice and participate, not only to authenticate the message of the Gospel, which is addressed as much to the whole man as to the whole world, but also to meet his own need for wholeness, which includes relaxation and participation in community life just as much as faithful churchgoing and morning devotions and dutiful work!

Missionaries have almost universally stayed out of the politics of their host country, even to the extent of rarely expressing any opinions on political events. Nationals themselves are divided on whether such self-imposed silence on the part of missionaries should obtain. Some feel they should choose up sides, particularly where government is corrupt or oppressive. The missionary, they insist, comes with a revolutionary message and belongs on the side of revolution. Others insist that he guard his foreignness, and "keep to religion." The danger in the first view is that the missionary may lose his own right to serve or impede the freedom of his national co-workers to propagate the Gospel. The danger in the second is that the church leaders who replace the missionary assume that non-involvement is the norm for Christians, so that they in turn lead their flocks in the path of non-participation in the nation's public life, to the impoverishment both of their message and of their nation. Both in political and non-political aspects of community and national life missionaries have unconsciously fostered the false dichotomy of the

religious and secular so characteristic of Western thought, something which Africans intuitively reject, since it is false to their
own view of being. To them neither national holidays nor political events are non-religious. "The important thing is that
every act of daily life has religious significance because through
it one may either maintain good relations with the gods or offend them with possibly disastrous results."[5]

Because Africans see life as a whole, they have an intuitive
interest in the politics of their nation and the world, since these
affect their daily life. They sense as well that their own acts of
worship in turn affect the destiny of their nation, indeed that
of the world. When Western fundamentalist missionaries bring a
narrow view which eschews political and social issues in favor of
"sticking to the Gospel" they are likely to be intuitively rejected. By the same token, the activist liberal missionary who
would submerge the church in social causes and eschew the
task of evangelism is likewise subject to instinctive rejection. As
Ralph Dodge suggests, "For Christianity to fail to embrace all
areas of life, as it proclaims its gospel, is a betrayal of its own authentic heritage and the best impulses of African religion."[6]

But beyond this falsification of life, and beyond segregation
itself, has been the actual destruction of whole cultures by the
impact of Western civilization. In this too the missionary has
shared. That he has contributed to the dramatic transformation
of millions of lives through the power of the Gospel he has
preached cannot be denied. It is equally obvious that he has been
largely responsible for victory over much that degraded human
life, as in the suppression of the slave trade, for example. But
he has not always been able to distinguish between the good and
the evil in the alien cultures to which he has brought the Good
News. And sometimes the Good News of salvation became in
his hands the bad news of deculturation. Rather than seeking
signs of God's providence in the mores of pagan society, he was

tempted to dismiss the whole as beyond redemption and sought to substitute the ways of his own people, concluding that what was good in a particular situation—his own—was universally good, indeed, the *only* universal good. Having come to teach, he assumed too often that there was nothing to learn.

Thus, not a few missionaries, for example, failed to learn the language of the people they had come to win to Christ, and thus failed at the basic level of communication. Unable to communicate adequately, they could hardly hope to appreciate the culture, even had they wished actually to penetrate it. While doing field research for a history of our mission work in Alaska, I found a poignant note, for example, in the records of the church in White Mountain, Alaska, written in limited English by the Eskimo recorder of the congregation. It read:

> Mrs. M. G. put up question in which I'm in favor of her idea. She said the older folks come to church, comes in, go out, without receiving anything that is very true. . . . No matter how we try to get away from Eskimo tongue, we can't get away from it, God has put every tongue and puts it on its place where no one is able to change. So members old folks they're hungry. And at least are the back-bone of our church.[7]

That was recorded in 1950. Our mission entered northwest Alaska in 1887. It was thought from the beginning more practical to teach the Eskimo English than to learn his difficult language with its several dialects. This decision was probably made in view of the fact that Alaska was American territory, and it was anticipated that English would replace the native tongues. That it would take three generations and longer to do so, and that the by-passed generations would therefore have to struggle along without the ready resources of the Bible to strengthen them, was not anticipated. In 1944 missionary Stanley Benson wrote: "The language barrier is a formidable hindrance to effective work from the pulpit."[8] And now, after more than eighty years of missionary effort among the Eskimo, our staff in Nome, Alaska, has found a sudden interest in learning conversational Eskimo. Too little, and too late!

There were other denials of culture by missionaries. A case in point is medicine. In his distaste for the superstition and magic of the witch doctor, the missionary rejected the indigenous herbalist, whose knowledge of plant alkaloids has helped primitive peoples survive the most unfavorable environments throughout the centuries. Now pharmaceutical teams from Europe and America send highly qualified research teams around the world in a crash effort to discover and investigate the values in time-honored herbs before this ancient wisdom becomes irrevocably lost.

So too with education. While primitive societies are often permissive in child-rearing, they have almost universally maintained systems of schooling for pre-adolescents where discipline is inculcated and tribal values taught through folk stories, myths, and proverbs, together with the arts and crafts of daily life. The Christian schools which have replaced them, while contributing much of good, have at the same time unquestionably undermined discipline and imbued students with disdain for the old ways. The new magic is the printed word, and the new fetish the *bic* (ball point pen), with which a man acquires the power to write.

In the area of family, Western missions almost without exception imposed monogamous marriage on polygamous societies from the outset, a disruptive decision, and one not unequivocably supported by Scripture. The effect was sometimes to drive out one devil only to fill the vacuum with seven worse—broken homes, juvenile delinquency, prostitution, increased venereal disease, sophistry, hypocrisy, rejection of the Gospel. Looking at the problem, Lesslie Newbigin writes:

> It has seemed that missions were trying to impose the rule of monogamy as a law before the conscience of African converts had awoken to the real issue, with the result that polygamy continues to flourish and the church seems often to represent rather the company of those who have managed to evade it, rather than the place where victory and joy are given by the Spirit in the life of the family.[9]

One could multiply the instances—the widespread rejection of native art forms and music for use in the church, the insistence on remarrying pagan couples converted to Christianity, even when their marriages had been obviously sanctioned by the community and blessed of God with many children, the arbitrary conferring of new names on new converts at baptism, and legalistic standards of conduct with American puritanical or European pietistic overtones imposed on new converts, with a consequent narrowing of the definition of sin in their minds—all of which had a way of saying that what is African is essentially bad.

Colin Turnbull, in his chilling book *The Lonely African*, describes in multiple real life illustrations how the destruction of the old traditional way has destroyed the moral foundations of the African's personal life. Since these foundations are structured in the extended family, its destruction results in the breakdown of the whole ancestral system, with a consequent terrible loneliness for the contemporary African. Having lost the right to join his ancestor, he finds he cannot join the new Western society in a real sense either. Writes Turnbull:

> The turning point was probably the realization that the meeting of the two worlds was not going to lead to a union

of mutual benefit through cooperation and mutual respect, but was going to involve the total destruction of
everything of importance to the African, including his beliefs, and result in a world primarily designed to benefit
the whites, and only incidentally perhaps the Africans.[10]

Kinshasa and other modern African cities present a strange
mixture of avid acceptance of Western culture and a reaffirmation of African values. It is evident in such symbols as dress,
the dance, music, and the arts. The minister driven about in his
Mercedes-Benz or Mark II complete with stereophonic record
player may sport native dress, or a Western business suit and
a leopard-skin cap. Hair straightening is passé. (Thank God! I
always felt a sense of revulsion at the slicked-down, straight
black hair affected by certain *évolués* during the colonial epoch.)
African women for their part may be seen with either authentic
African and neo-African coiffures, or European swept-up
bouffantes. Continues Turnbull:

> So long as the West African maintained his political hostil-
> ity he felt free to adopt the white man's ways as nearly
> completely as he could. But in so doing he convinced
> himself that he had no need of the past, that he was, in fact,
> Westernized. It is only now, perhaps, after several years of
> increasing independence that he is beginning to realize that
> he has left something of real worth behind. . . .
>   There are some who feel they are losing nothing; oth-
> ers feel that they are merely losing their self-respect in this
> wholehearted denial of the past. But there are many who
> see very clearly that they are losing the things they need to
> give life a meaning beyond the narrow meaning of national-
> ism or westernization, and yet can see no room for tradi-
> tional life in the unbelieving world into which they have
> been born. For many of them, Christianity is, at best, a
> very temporary and very local anesthetic.[11]

So there is also, therefore, the *legacy of the continuing present*, a legacy being created currently in daily acts that color the relationships of black and white. It is a legacy of suspicion and fear, hesitation and mistrust, distance and resentment, guilt and doubt, continued segregation and discrimination, happily diminishing in a growing number of places, but remaining in others to haunt those yearning for genuine communication. Ought we really be surprised when a former clerk once known to whites only as Pierre and now become an important government official makes the white man go to the end of the line at the post office, or insists on some minor technicality to delay a visa application, or leaves the contents of the newly arrived missionary's suitcase in disarray after a thorough customs inspection? Are we to wonder that a group of soldiers sporting powerful weapons should halt a white man's truck for a fancied violation of the law and subject him to indignities? Is it inexplicable that the captain of the ferry which a missionary hastens to catch before dark should decide that no more trips are to be made that day although there is still light enough for two more trips?

For scores of years the African stood at the end of the line, was subject to police power, and submitted to curfews based on his color. The schoolteacher who now acts as customs agent at the frontier may have been mercilessly humiliated before his classmates at a mission school for having neglected his classes because clan pressures required him to attend a distant funeral. The former nurse now installed as governor of the province may have been called *nyama!* (animal) by the very Portuguese trader seeking an extension of his franchise.

To deny this legacy in these days of African autonomy and independence, when Africans have won their freedom and the recognition of peopleness, is to deceive ourselves. It is seen, on the one hand, in gestures of assertiveness on the part of Africans in their relations with Europeans, and in the quasi-paranoid defenses of the European against this assertiveness on the other. It is apparent in the gravitation of whites to other whites, whites formerly in little relation to each other—Catholic priests and Protestant missionary, Belgian doctor and Portuguese trader, Flemish and Walloon—in a thirst for protective togetherness. Even the token integration of the mission compound, and the turning over of mission institutions to African management does not alter *ipso facto* the basic pattern of white-black relations. While in most instances church and mission have become structurally one, and in some, dynamically one as well, in too many the basic structure still persists of two communities operating separately, ostensibly mission and church, but for all practical purposes (and certainly psychologically) white and black. There are frequent meetings at the top echelons and at the grass roots, and even moments of true oneness, but the general pattern of communication in such instances perpetuates that obtaining in the colonial era: The mission council (white) meets separately and makes recommendations to the church council (black), and vice versa.

Where this pattern persists it appears to the African as a subtle rejection of his adulthood, an affront to his dignity, and an effort to hold him back from true equality. All divisions today are interpreted racially and all resistance to what Africans want is seen simply as a continued attempt by the white man to restrict the black and to deny him the powers which the white man has at his disposal. To resist the formation of a nurses' training school or the development of a university desired by the African community, however sound the reason in a given circumstance, is interpreted by the African as our saying: "You are black and higher education really isn't for you."

In Alan Paton's *Cry, the Beloved Country* the old African Msimangu expresses his apprehension about the future of white-black relations in these words: "I have one great fear in my heart, that one day when they turn to loving they will find we are turned to hating."[12] The remarkable thing is that "when Congo burst its seams"[13] there was not more of rape and murder and beatings. Rather, there remains a substantial pool of good will toward the white missionary in Africa. It is there because of the grace of God and Africa's own graciousness. And it is there because there is another legacy besides the legacy of barriers.

Chapter 3
_____

IS THE CRY CONTEMPORARY?

Granted that there *is* anti-missionary sentiment in many parts of the world—both in the receiving and sending areas—is the cry "Missionary, Go Home!" a current one? Or in facing this problem are we guilty, as we too often are, of trying to answer questions that aren't being asked? Are people really saying this, or are we simply echoing a cry once heard, trying to be "with it," carried by the inertia of a spent force? Is the cry indeed contemporary? Let us look at the evidence.

I have thrice been present as a resident in a revolutionary country during a revolution, and twice I have visited in countries that had just been subjected to attempted coups. Through these experiences and fairly extensive travels I have had personal opportunity to sense at first hand whether the sentiment "Missionary, Go Home!" is real or imagined, or real but overplayed.

One recent such experience was in Kinshasa, capital of the Democratic Republic of the Congo. I had returned with my family for a nine-month re-immersion overseas after five years in the homeland in mission administration. On the morning of August 13, 1967, just a few hours after our arrival, I went to the American Embassy to register our return with my own government. Suddenly a mob materialized in front of the Embassy, from nowhere, swirling, shouting, threatening. I watched helplessly as a Volkswagen was forced to a stop on the street in front of the building and the driver slumped forward in his seat from a blow to the head by a two-by-four thrust through his windshield. And I quickly retreated from view as a rock burst through the window of the reception room.

It was not an anti-missionary demonstration. It was hardly even anti-American. The mob had pursued a Belgian couple who sought refuge in our embassy after their own was sacked and burned, and quickly dispersed when President Mobutu suddenly appeared and dismissed them. But I felt uneasy then, and was aware of a vague sense of hostility when, a few hours later, I joined some friends in a bit of downtown shopping. And little wonder that there was hostility—the mercenaries who had only a couple of days before taken over Bukavu made all of us with white skin suspect.

Two days after the Kinshasa episode a mob reacted in Gemena in the Ubangi, the very area for which we were heading. A white trader was killed, and whites in general menaced. A missionary teacher at a home economics school in the city was shielded from harm, when trapped in her Volkswagen, by an African who recognized her. But another was included among the three prizes which the mob had in mind to seize as they thronged before the gates of the agricultural school, where they were fortunately stopped by the Congolese Army. They had come, a chastened and frightened missionary staff learned later, "to get the cow, the rabbits, and so-and-so" (naming a particular missionary).

At the moment of our return, were the Congolese saying, "Missionary, Go Home!"? It rather looked that way!

We were headed for the post of Wasolo, a name that leaped into headlines the world over in November 1964, when Dr.

Paul Carlson was taken from the mission hospital there by a rebel band and brought to Kisangani, where he died with fifty others in a hail of bullets from machine guns moments before Belgian paratroopers effected a rescue of the white hostages. He was one of more than 120 Christian missionaries, Catholic and Protestant, who have died in recent years in the Congo alone for their faith. And voices are still raised in the Congo against missionaries, as observers and delegates to the annual meeting of the Congo Protestant Council learned in March 1969 in Kinshasa. These events lend substance to the impression of many visitors to lands where missionaries still function, that as a group they are the last of a (generally) noble line, who haven't yet got the message, or who refuse to read it.

The Boxer Rebellion in China happened too long ago to be fresh in the memory of moderns. But most are familiar with Lederer and Burdick's *The Ugly American*,[1] with its suggestion that Americans are an unwanted breed in much of the world (and often deservedly so, they imply). Their book about overseas Americans in general was followed by Bishop Ralph Dodge's volume on missionaries in particular, entitled *The Unpopular Missionary*,[2] based largely on the Bishop's experiences in the Congo and Rhodesia. James Scherer in turn, writing from a background in Asia, contributed the title *Missionary, Go Home!*[3] After the second widespread evacuation of missionaries from the Congo in 1964 Levi Keidel wrote in the Mennonite publication *Congo News* an article captioned "Shall We Call It Quits?" And as recently as March 1968 *World Vision Magazine* carried the title "Should Missionaries Get Out of the Philippines?" A substantial segment of the world feels that the answer to both of the last questions is an affirmative. Certain governments have already taken steps to restrict the influx of Christian missionaries into their countries. The government of India, for example, adopted regulations in 1954 limiting the number of mis-

sionaries who could enter the country. At that time it was decided to permit entry visas only for those who came to fill positions for which no Indians were available. And although Indian
churches by special representations to government officials have
continued to obtain entry permits for missionaries in a variety
of kinds of work, government ministers repeatedly remind them
that the right of entry is a courtesy extended by themselves
to foreign missionaries, and that they expect Indian Christians
to take over responsibility for all mission activity in India eventually, and the more rapidly the better. In 1965 these rules were
extended to missionaries from the Commonwealth nations, which
had previously enjoyed special concessions. In July of 1967
the Indian government suddenly ordered all foreign missionaries to leave the area north of the Brahmaputra River in Assam.
Strong representations from the regional Protestant Council and
the Roman Catholic Church led the home ministry in Delhi to
reconsider certain cases, but the order itself was not rescinded.
Religious News Service reported that nearly eighty missionaries
were informed that their residence permits would not be renewed
on expiration. Others (from America and Canada) were expelled prior to expiration of their visas. According to the *Christian Times*, out of 5,000 missionaries in India, some 80 Catholics
and 170 others who had applied for visa renewal in the first half
of 1968 had been refused.[4]

So marked for a time was the acceleration of the campaign
against U.S. missionaries that Ambassador Chester Bowles felt
impelled to declare that the charges made against missionaries
(revolutionary activity) were pure invention. At the time he
spoke out, reported the *Christian Century*, "relief programs
sponsored by voluntary organizations were providing daily meals
for 4½ million children and 4 million adults. In addition, their
representatives had built some 200 miles of roads, helped erect
about 100 miles of dams, and dug or deepened 343 wells and 90

reservoirs."[5] It was therefore perhaps natural that Ambassador Bowles should officially reflect a deep American sense of disgust.

Not only in Asia, but in Africa as well, certain countries have made it clear that they no longer welcome Christians as missionaries. The Sudan, a Muslim country, has perhaps been the most explicit. By 1964 all missionaries had been expelled, with the exception of a few in the Khartoum area, who, it is suspected, were allowed to continue to work as exhibits to the world of the regime's "religious tolerance." As this is written the only relaxation of the strict regulations imposed on foreign Christians has been to permit two African Catholic priests to enter the country in 1968.

But the cry "Missionary, Go Home!" does not come only from the lips of those countries grown weary of being regarded as "mission fields." Some of its most vocal exponents are home-based. A Catholic University missions expert, for example, addressing 1,000 delegates representing more than 200 American Catholic mission-sending societies during the Mission Secretariat's meeting in Washington, D.C., in September 1967, declared flatly that Roman Catholic missionaries should pack up their bags, dismantle the missions structure, and start "humanizing" mankind through secular evolution. The era of the foreign missionary, he insisted, is gone forever. "Missionary, Go Home!"[6]

He was recently joined by a Protestant theologian, Dr. Frederick Dale Bruner, writing in the *Christian Century* under the title "The American Missionary Problem—An Essay in Conscience." Writing out of a Philippine context Dr. Bruner states in his opening paragraph:

The continuing presence of American missionaries in the Philippines poses an ever more acute problem of conscience for both Filipino Christians and the missionaries themselves. This problem may serve as a paradigm of the situation pe-

culiar to the Christian missionary enterprise today. At the
same time, it may illumine the larger problem of the American presence in Asia and the Third World generally. Put
succinctly, the problem is that American missionaries are
inhibiting and impeding the wholesome, natural growth of
an indigenous and responsible Philippine Christianity—in
spite of the fact that they came to the islands not to hinder
the Philippine church but to help it. The difference between purpose and result heightens the tensions between
native and American Christians today. Indeed, lines are
drawn not only between Filipinos but between Americans
as well.[7]

Dr. Bruner takes pains to insist that he speaks only of the
Philippine situation, which he knows first hand, and only for
American Protestants, though he admits that part of what he
has to say would apply as well to other foreign, white missionaries, including Roman Catholics.

He further limits his critique by stating that he speaks as an
"institutional" as distinguished from a "field" missionary; i.e., as
a teacher in urban schools rather than a worker in the "bush."
But such restrictions aside, there is little question that he speaks
for a growing number of thoughtful missionaries currently engaging in deep soul-searching on the issue of their continued
presence in foreign lands.

The problem, as Bruner sees it, is that large-scale subsidiza-
tion by American funds is the rule rather than the exception in
Protestant institutions in the Philippines. "The inevitable result
is that able Filipino Christians are made to appear unattractively
dependent and American Christians unattractively benevolent—
the 'spiritual problem' underlying all other, more obvious problems of the American mission."[8]

In many lands the unfortunate consequence of such over-
whelming American presence is an "abrasive counterreaction" in

the form of nationalism. What disturbs Bruner is that in the Philippines it evokes rather more decidedly an unnatural dependence. "The Filipino Protestant is in danger of being unmanned. His praise of America and Americans may be—often is—sincere, but inevitably it smells of dollars. He fears that without American help the institution could not exist, and he knows that at present its operation greatly depends on the continuing inflow of American men and money. This inflow appears to require of Filipino Christian leaders a reciprocal outflow of praise and thanks."[9]

The fact that an institution may be extensively Filipinized (or Zambianized, or *Congolizé*) in respect to its leadership, faculty, and board does not change the essential picture. For the problem is money.

> Money talks, and the recipients, of course, listen. That an institution reacts gratefully to American help is not necessarily a sign of weakness. Gratitude can be the most admirable of traits. But when gratitude must be cultivated over more than half a century with no end yet in sight, when the recipient must constantly render thanks for the blessings bestowed on him, it is difficult to evade the conviction that continual American giving (well-intentioned though it may be) and continual Philippine receiving (grateful as it is) has crippled important segments of Philippine Christianity.[10]

The issue for sensitive Christians is "whether to lose their identity or dollars; to gain self-respect or to have a well-equipped institution. Some, it would seem, are ready to stand up and serve notice that they are no longer willing to bend the grateful knee."[11]

Bruner insists that the financial loss which would be incurred by a true declaration of independence on the part of the

Filipino church would be only temporary. He points to the generally acknowledged fact that those churches which have had
the least outside support from the West have been the fastest-
growing (e.g., the Pentecostal churches of Chile and Brazil).
He argues that there is plenty of Philippine money available,
but that few well-to-do Filipinos feel the need to contribute so
long as American money continues to flow. Filipino churches
have a low sense of stewardship simply because they have not had
to support their own institutions. The obvious need, therefore, is
to withdraw American Christian help.

Withdrawal is, of course, hard to effect. The plant and
the program are there, and the desire to help, from the American
side, is there. The Filipinos, on their side, are bound by Asian
courtesy and Christian grace not to ask their benefactors with
whom they have been so long associated to go. While they may
politely be saying, "We still need your help," they may not really
mean it. They may actually be saying, "Please go!"

But withdrawal, for all that, Bruner insists, is necessary. It
is necessary not only for the good of the Filipino church. It is
equally necessary for the good of the American. For "when one
is on the giving end over a long period of time it is very difficult
to avoid feeling a little superior, consciously or unconsciously.
This is neither attractive nor Christian. Too much giving swells
the ego of the giver."[12]

Bruner is willing that a token American missionary presence
be maintained, "to symbolize and to help realize the ecumenical,
fraternal, and supranational character of the Christian church."
But it must be token. For a faculty of an educational institution
to be just under half American is not a sufficient reduction.
Americans are aggressive by nature and any substantial American presence is *ipso facto* a quorum. For Filipinos to find their
own soul the American presence must be reduced to a minimum.
Filipinos are, in consequence of the American presence, too

Americanized already, Bruner maintains. Their students are full of American information. The sermons and speeches of their clergy and speakers are full of American quotations—from Norman Vincent Peale, Bishop Sheen, John F. Kennedy, and others. These are signs of an insidious deculturation, "the American mongrelization of a great Asian people," one of the most serious evidences of which is the much-discussed "brain drain" of Filipino leadership from the Philippines to America.

For Filipinos to find and be themselves, in the life of the church as well as the nation, there must be a "drastic reduction of the American presence in all its forms," if the Filipinos are to escape from "spiritual thralldom to the United States of America." The American military and business communities, Bruner admits, are not likely to hear or heed his plea. Therefore, he concludes, a substantial number of American missionaries ought to leave the islands at once.

> Is there any less drastic way of serving the Philippine soul? I would genuinely like to know. For as a citizen of a rich nation I cannot fully justify large-scale abandonment of a developing nation. On the contrary. I am sure that we have an obligation toward those in need of whatever help we can give. After all, the Good Samaritan did not advise the stricken wayfarer to help himself for integrity's sake. But the Philippine church, for which and to which I speak here in particular, is not stricken—unless, paradoxically, its better parts are suffering under the bear-hug help of its American Samaritan.[13]

Bruner is not alone in his "agonizing reappraisal" of a continued missionary presence, as we have already seen, nor is the problem limited to the Philippines. For historic reasons, the Philippine situation is perhaps unique. But the problem is universal.

The *La Jolla Presbyterian* reported, for example, the departure of an American couple from Iran, who left because of "the feeling, shared by many other missionaries, that there is a need for the Iranians to be free to establish their own church, without the confusion and conflicting influences of foreign personnel, programs and money."[14] In Taiwan, during a visit to that mission-laden island made in March 1969, I heard this sentiment, expressed by a disillusioned Chinese national Christian, and conveyed by a disturbed missionary: "There are scores of missionaries in Taiwan whose only function is to channel money."

One could multiply these examples, from nearly every quarter of the globe which the sending West has traditionally regarded as "mission fields." But the examples given suffice to make the point. And it is not a point that we are concerned to make. It may indeed have already been made too well. We reiterate it only to admit a fact of our times. And having admitted it, we may do well to re-examine the evidence a bit to discern if the cry "Missionary, Go Home!" is truly directed at the sent of the Evangel. I think we should have to admit in the first place that sometimes the cry is more accurately to be heard as "Yankee, Go Home!," with the missionary sharing only incidentally in the clamor, a victim of his American nationality. Yankee-baiting is a popular international sport, hardly limited to the Third World. Where scapegoats are needed, the missionary cannot always hope to escape the burden of his nationality, though it is amazing how discriminating the newly independent nations have been for the most part. Certainly the Congolese people, in the years just past when repeated turmoil has favored the tendency to lump all whites in a category labeled "dangerous to the national security," have largely judged missionaries on the degree to which they had individually communicated a personal concern for the people among whom they lived. An obvious exception was the rebellion of 1964, where missionaries ultimately became targets as a class of the revolution. But that was only in the late stages, and even then individual rebel officers took great pains to protect particular missionaries, often at great risk to themselves. One such instance known to me personally involved a subordinate of Christophe Gbenye, the rebel commander. An officer of high rank in the rebel army, he personally escorted Reverend Paul Hanson, a Norwegian Baptist missionary, over a considerable distance across the border to safety in the Central African Republic. And external forces, it must also be remembered, entered the Congo picture to make it atypical.

The problem in India to which we referred above had clear political overtones, not specifically related to the question of missionary presence *per se*. In the state of Nagaland the government leaders and more than half the population are Christian and have long demanded a separate state outside the Indian nation, at times engaging in underground revolutionary activity to forward their goals. When a truce was arranged between the chief minister of Assam and the dissident Christians, the Anglican priest who represented them (widely known for his efforts on behalf of the people of South Africa) plainly showed a partisan attitude in favor of the rebel Nagas, with the result that Christian missionaries as a group suffered. Many Hindu leaders, and the government in Delhi, related the political unrest to the fact that its perpetrators were Christian, and suspected foreign missionaries of complicity at the least, and of active instigation in some instances.

When as a consequence the government of India intensified its restrictions against U.S. missionaries and Ambassador Chester Bowles reacted with some vigor in their defense, he raised the specter of Communist activity, aimed at destroying cooperation between India, the United States, and voluntary organizations to relieve Indians who are victims of famine. While missionaries and their supporters are well advised not to see red flags in every event that threatens their mission, it is clear that international communism by its own admission is committed to the destruction of the Christian mission. Certainly it was a major element in the rebellion of 1964 in the Congo. And it can at least be expected to swell the volume of the cry "Missionary, Go Home!" wherever it has the opportunity, when not directly responsible for initiating or fomenting it. Thus the missionary may in some instances be a victim not only of anti-Americanism or of the particular nationalism of the country where he witnesses, but even of the Cold War. And not to see and admit this is to give unjust and false content to the anti-missionary sentiment expressed in particular instances.

Again, the Western missionary is generally white. As such he is caught up in the arena of the current racial struggle. He may share—and too often has shared in the past—the prejudices of his culture. But he may also not only be free of them, but be in the vanguard of those for whom color is no barrier to human fellowship, and yet suffer rejection by people of color for the simple reason that he lacks it. That is to say, the cry "Missionary, Go Home!" may more accurately be heard as "Whitey, Go Home!" and the missionary may participate in its onus quite incidentally, in a way unrelated to his missionary activity. He cannot deny his whiteness, nor the meaning of it for him, as we have clearly seen in the preceding chapters. Yet to accept the cry "Missionary, Go Home!" at face value, i.e., directed against the missionary as a missionary *per se*, is to do violence to the facts and to ignore an important element in the contemporary content of the cry.

And he is Western, with all which that implies. Part of the content is surely a protest against Western civilization, its materialism, its dichotomization of the sacred and the secular, its exploitation of nature, its haste and discourtesy, its terrifying efficiency, its capacity for waste and destruction, its ostentation, its confusing paradoxes of enormous good and enormous evil, of simultaneous concern and disregard for life. The missionary cannot divorce himself from his association with the West, even should he wish to do so. What is important here is that we recognize again that the cry "Missionary, Go Home!" is not often clearly a protest against the Christian message nor its messenger; that there is a sense in which the missionary is innocent; that he is caught in the dilemma of simultaneously bearing in his body the marks of the Lord Jesus and the mark of the beastly in his own heritage.

Finally, in the echoes from the homeland, not all of the chorus is motivated by concern for the well-being of the overseas church. One senses on the part of some critics of overseas mission an almost unseemly eagerness to have it come to an end. At the worst it reflects a growing isolationism resurging in our country as a consequence of increasing weariness at being the world's whipping boy in seeming ingratitude for all America has done for the world, and contains elements of the vindictive. At best it is the product of a considered judgment that we have been generous abroad to the extent of neglecting problems at home; that we have, for example, fed India's millions while ignoring the poverty of 30,000,000 Americans; that we have built fine schools and hospitals for Africans while scorning the educational and health needs of Afro-Americans. Yet, as Barnerd M. Luben reminded us in a speech given in New York: "The poor people of America can march on Washington. The poor people of the rest of the world are dying at the rate of six a minute. They can't march; they can't even stand up."[15]

And one can further counter by insisting that our national foreign aid program does not yet approach the one per cent of our gross national product recommended by the World Council of Churches and the United Nations, and that we spend less on overseas mission than entertainment or tobacco. The fact is that a nation able to continue to prosper while simultaneously supporting a $50 billion annual bill for armaments, a $30 billion annual bill for war in Viet-Nam, and a massive program in outer space is quite capable, given the will to do so, of sustaining a simultaneous attack on poverty at home and abroad, without jeopardizing the efforts of voluntary agencies, including the church, or its own welfare.

The truth is that the church in America is spending less and less on overseas mission and more and more on itself, as Dr. Luben further noted. My own church, a small denomination (67,000 members) with a reputation for being "mission-minded" and "stewardship-conscious" doubled its income for all causes (from $7 million to $14 million) in the six years between 1960 and 1966. During that period the overseas missionary staff dropped from 150 to 130, and the budget for overseas mission remained static (an equal drop, from the effects of inflation). The denomination's major educational institution in the meantime doubled its facilities, many large and beautiful churches were built, numerous retirement centers were established, summer camp facilities mushroomed, and regional conferences and national headquarters increased their staffs. One sometimes gets the feeling that there are pastors and lay leaders in the church who would actually welcome a demise of overseas mission, whose glamor they feel has had a competitive advantage over local programs, in order that they might have more resources for their own favorite projects—often equally deserving, but sometimes mere reflections of the pressures of American affluence for improvements in the church that are essentially material.

To the extent that we recognize these overtones, we do well to hear and listen to the cry "Missionary, Go Home!" But we do ill to turn up the volume or be confused by the static and the jamming.

Part 11

Missionary, Come Back!

Chapter 4

THE OTHER SIDE OF THE COIN

In Chapter One we revisited in memory the Democratic Republic of the Congo, that interesting central African country so frequently torn by strife, and so thoroughly penetrated by Christian missionaries in the course of its pre-colonial, colonial, and post-colonial history.

Recently I revisited the Congo in actuality, spending some nine months there, including several weeks in the capital of Kinshasa as well as other urban centers, such as Mbandaka, capital of the province of the Equator, and Kisangani, made famous as Stanleyville, focus of revolutionary activity the past several years, and now hosting the nation's third university, the Free University of the Congo.

My travels took me from Kimpese in the lower Congo to Nyankunde, close to the Uganda border in the east, and included Bondo in the north where Christophe Gbenye conceived the idea of using Christian missionaries as hostages in a last desperate attempt to save his crumbling empire at the time of the Simba rebellion in 1964.

Most of my time was spent in the Ubangi-Mongala region of the northwest Congo, true bush country boasting no impressive urban centers. I functioned in part as a mission executive, helping missionary staff and national church leaders work out new mission-church relationships, and observing the church at work. I also functioned simply as a missionary doctor again at the somewhat isolated post of Wasolo where Dr. Paul Carlson served in a brief missionary career that ended in martyrdom.

On the basis of my experience of re-immersion as a missionary on the Congo scene, as well as observations from visits of several weeks' duration in several lands of Asia and Latin America, I want to suggest that the cry "Missionary, Go Home!," though genuine, sometimes vociferous, and, in certain instances undoubtedly deserving of an affirmative response is not the only cry. For there is another cry, equally poignant, uttered not only from the throats but the breasts of large masses of people in the developing nations, and it declares just as earnestly, "Missionary, Come Back!"

This plea may well have been missed by some whose surveys have been limited to a few interviews in the nations' capitals and who have taken neither the time nor the trouble to talk with pastors, lay ministers, catechists, deacons, and ordinary church members in the grass roots, confining their conversations to vocal leaders jealous of their new-found selfhood and in a phase of overreaction, or to secretaries in offices resentful (often justly, but as often unjustly) of a continued missionary presence. Just as the secular press headlines a can of red paint thrown by a handful of youths against the car of the President of the United States as the measure of his reception by a Central American country and ignores the bigger fact that he was actually joyously and enthusiastically received by the masses of that country, so the religious press, yielding to the current mood of self-recrimination and hand-wringing, often takes the word of a few vocal and volatile spokesmen of the emerging churches in developing countries as the true index of the missionary's reception in those lands, ignoring the deep pool of desire on the part of masses of common churchmen as well as non-churchmen in those countries for the missionary's return. It is only fair that we come to the defense of that host of dedicated people we call missionaries who, although they may not always understand in depth the full meaning of the events which swirl about them, are nonetheless willing to be where the action is, often at great personal cost. There is something almost revolting about an authoritative judgment passed by someone who makes a forty-eight-hour or even two-week visit to a land torn by revolution and then returns to the security of his home base to make a severe judgment from a posture of non-involvement on those who are deeply involved. This is no plea against criticism. It is only to suggest that it is better made and certainly better received when it is the considered judgment of those who face their problems and fears on the field of action.

Missionaries continue to be wanted, loved, and even liked in much of the world. Their departure in many places has been an event of great sadness to the communities they have left. William J. Petersen, author of the book *Another Hand on Mine*, the story of Dr. Carl Becker of the African Inland Mission, tells how, during the tragic turmoil and prodigious pressures of rebellion in the Congo—events fully as threatening to Congolese Christians as to their white co-believers—the Africans pleaded with Dr. Becker and his colleagues not to leave them.[1] This story was repeated often in countless scenes in the northeastern Congo and the Kwilu where the rebel threat to the lives of missionaries forced their evacuation. Delbert A. Kuehl, executive assistant director of The Evangelical Alliance Mission, in reviewing the Becker biography for *Christianity Today*, states it as his opinion that "those closely involved in worldwide missions realize that this is the general picture and 'missionary, go home,' the exception."[2]

The May 12, 1968 issue of the *Christian Times* reported from Addis Ababa that the Ethiopian Ministry of Education had appealed to the Sudan Interior Mission not to close its Silti station, 125 miles south of Addis. Closure of the station, prompted by a shortage of personnel and unresponsiveness to the Gospel, triggered an unexpected reaction. The local people, formerly indifferent, petitioned the authorities to request the return of the missionaries. A new contract was thereupon negotiated and two missionaries appointed in response to the appeal.[3]

The same journal reports a similar event from quite a different quarter of the globe—Mexico. Its August 18, 1968 issue carries a story from San Juan Coatzospam, where officials recently sent an urgent message to the Wycliffe Director in Mexico, Dr. Frank Robbins, requesting the return of Janet Turner, a nurse, and Priscilla Small, "her secretary," Wycliffe translators to 1,800 Highland Mixtec Indians. The article reads:

> When Janet and Priscilla first went to San Juan, they spent their first nights listening to bullets skim across the roof of their rented house. Four years of patience and practical help caused the president of the village who allowed the shooting to write this letter:
> "Please send the girls back. (They had left for consultation on their translation). They are the only ones who know what medicines will save our children. They are the only ones who know how to treat us. We asked the state capital at our market town for help, but they couldn't come. Please, send the nurse and the nurse's secretary back to us."[4]

The girls did return and, working twelve hours a day for a month, stopped an epidemic that had taken the lives of sixty-seven children in two months. When they left for furlough, men of the village gave them a tape. "This is a message from us to your President of the United States," they said. "We just want to thank your President for sending you to us." One may be tempted to smile at their naïveté, and to dismiss this and similar events as a bit corny, but their very naïveté and corniness is a refreshing antidote to the cynicism which is occasionally the main source of strength for the cry "Missionary, Go Home!"

Our own experience in returning to a Congo from which we had been absent for five years was similar. I mentioned earlier the hostility we had sensed in Kinshasa during the weeks of mercenary occupation of several Congolese cities in the eastern part of the country. In Kinshasa I was a statistic, an unknown white face. The story was quite different where we were recognized and remembered.

When we flew up-country to Gemena from Kinshasa we got out at Libenge on the northern frontier because a heavy rainstorm made landing at Gemena improbable. None of the missionary staff was there to meet us, and no white man met the plane. The crowd of Africans who met it stared in curiosity at this crazy missionary family coming into the area when all other European traffic at the moment was in the opposite direction. The Congolese customs officer recognized me as the physician who had stayed on in the Yakoma area when the Belgians left in 1960, and had joined the staff of the local government hospital in Banzyville to work for the infant republic, and he greeted me and my family with joy. The local pastor of the Church of Christ in the Ubangi recognized us too, brought us fresh bread to still our hunger, and helped us secure the services of a Congolese merchant who was willing to drive us to the nearest mission station.

Later we returned to Wasolo at a time when white mercenaries were killing Congolese para-commandos in Bukavu and tensions were high, and we got a glorious welcome. There where no missionary had been stationed for four years (since Dr. Carlson's death) and throughout the Ubangi in the west, on across the width of the Congo from Kimpese to Kisangani, on east to the border at Nyankunde, and north to Bondo—throughout a broad area, some of it ravaged in turn by rebels and mercenaries and the national army—the message that came through loud and clear was "Missionary, Come Back!"

I would be the first to admit that the cry cannot be taken simply at face value. Bush people like those to whom we returned may have many mixed reasons for the missionary's return. Simple nostalgia is certainly a part of it. The return of the missionary can be a symbol of the good old days when there was constant security, trucks to ride in, hospitals and dispensaries with adequate supplies of drugs, schools with plenty of chalk and notebooks, the excitement of a busy and humming mission enterprise. The missionary often meant a supply of trade goods, and building a dispensary or a school or a church or a house or an airstrip gave employment to a lot of local labor.

Once the initial flush of excitement over becoming a free people is passed, there may even be some wistfulness for the old *patron*, dispensing not only rides and work and drugs and books, but an aura of predictability in an ordered universe. Church leaders plagued with problems of discipline may actually wish for the return of the benign judge and policeman who, when all else failed, would give the final word and settle the matter.

But, admitting all of this, we should be guilty of mere cynicism if we were to say that the story ends there. There is more than nostalgia in the cry. There is more than a wistful desire for security and predictability. There is more than a hope for employment or an adequate supply of medicines or books. There is a deep recognition that Christ reconciles men at a time when the mass media cry daily about racial and class conflict, and a hope for a visible symbol of this reconciliation in the presence of a missionary in the midst of the pagan non-believers who surround the believer. There is an earnest desire for help and counsel from someone who is recognized as having lived longer in the tradition of the faith than themselves. There is a kind of foreboding in the face of a technological explosion which is enveloping this world which the African and Asian and Latin American feels, and at least a grudging recognition that the presence of representatives of those who have authored this technological revolution may somehow help them better to weather the storm.

No, the cry "Missionary, Come Back!" is a genuine cry, sometimes superficial as we have seen, but more often deep and even desperate. It was clearly expressed on repeated occasions during our stay in the Congo by President Mobutu, the Minister of Agriculture Mr. Litho, the Governor of the Equator Mr. Mukamba, on down to the lowliest local official and tribal chief. It was affirmed by Dr. Pierre Shaumba, then secretary general of the Congo Protestant Council, and Pastor Zacharie Alenge, president of the Church of Christ in the Ubangi, as well as by a deacon of the local church in the village of Wapinda, and by the villagers of that and countless other villages, whether lisping child or budding student or failing patriarch or barren wife.

It might be expected in the Congo, where the rebellion destroyed hospitals and schools and decimated the indigenous leadership which emerged from mission schools to lead the nation at all levels after independence came abruptly in 1960. Thus Archbishop Augustun Fataki recently left Kisangani to tour Europe and North America seeking to fill vacancies in his archdiocese. Similarly from Upper Volta, Paul Cardinal Zoungrana, Archbishop of Ouagadougou, visited Paris and noted that the native clergy of Africa are not numerous enough to minister to the continent's new Christians.

But the cry is not limited to Congo and Africa, as we have already seen. The rapidly growing church of Indonesia is in desperate need of pastoral helpers from overseas to augment its own inadequate resources in personnel. It is recognized by national Christian leadership that unless help is secured from Christians abroad, and soon, much of the harvest may be lost by reversion to the past, or to quasi-Christian sects. Wherever there are sheep without shepherds one hears the cry "Missionary, Come Back!" And where there are shepherds whose flocks are too large for adequate pasturing and watering, the cry is also heard. The half-million-member Minahasa Church of the Northern Celebes, with whom the Church of the Brethren, the Disciples of Christ, the Evangelical Covenant Church, and recently (in renewed relationship) the Reformed Church of the Netherlands have all had fruitful and mutually delightful fraternal relations, asked me on a recent visit (March 1969), if we couldn't supply teachers for their University and Theological School in Tomohon. Previously our own involvement had been limited to supplying two doctors for the staff of the Bethesda Hospital in Tomohon. Dominie Luntungan, the head of the church, speaking for the executive council of the synod which welcomed me to one of its sessions, spoke warmly of the services performed by our missionary representatives and of the rich fellowship our association of seven years had engendered, and declared with the assent of all present that they would welcome missionaries who would serve in the schools, in, as he put it, "joint action for mission."

The church of central Java, whose fantastic growth has been reported in many journals[5] recognizes the need of help in teaching the thousands of former Communists and Muslims who have come to faith in Christ in the last two or three years, and has accepted missionaries from Britain and Holland to help in the work of training laymen in the church so as to reap the full harvest.

And the cry is heard not only abroad in places of need. In the same circles where strong voices insist that missionaries pack their bags and come home, equally concerned voices insist that the day of the missionary is *not* over. On the contrary, his opportunities were never greater!

In the meeting of the same Mission Secretariat in Washington to which we referred earlier, where it was declared that the era of the foreign missionary was gone forever by the Reverend Ronan Hoffman, associate professor of missiology at the Catholic University, another spokesman rose to disagree sharply. He was Catholic convert Avery Dulles, professor of systematic theology at Woodstock (Maryland) College and son of the late Secretary of State John Foster Dulles. "The Christian missionary effort should not be dismantled but greatly intensified," insisted Professor Dulles, "to assist in the conversion of men to God in Christ and to gather them together into the one Church."[6] He pointed out huge areas of the globe which the Gospel has not yet penetrated, and while admitting with Hoffman that "ours is a revolutionary era," he cautioned, "I should be very much afraid of any revolution which attempted to achieve the true good of humanity apart from the knowledge and love of God in Jesus Christ."[7]

The debate in Protestant circles takes a similar tack. Thus, in response to Dr. Frederick Dale Bruner's article in the June 5, 1968, *Christian Century*, to which we gave considerable space above, Mr. Nene Ramientos, associate director for the Asia–South Pacific Congress on Evangelism and editor of *Crusader Magazine*, writes a rebuttal in the November 1968 issue of *World Vision Magazine*.

Mr. Ramientos begins by admitting that some Filipinos are completely disenchanted with foreign missionaries and advocate absolute severance of ties with people from the West. In addition, others who seem inspired by purely nationalistic motives, favor withdrawal of their missionary colleagues and the complete turnover of the work of the church and its institutions to the na-

tionals. But others disagree, he points out. Among them are those
who "would not want anything done in their relationship with
missionaries which might be detrimental to their corporate witness before the community."[8] Among them also, admittedly, are
those "who prefer prudence in the midst of a situation where
admittedly the national-missionary relationship is less than wholesome or desirable."[9] But the fact "that there have been some irri-
tants in the relationship between missionaries and nationals is no
valid reason for terminating the relationship."[10] It is easy enough
for a national determined to do so, he continues, to make a "lit-
any of 'sins of the ugly missionary.' "[11] Certainly the foreign missionary has done many things that have caused strain in his relationship with national Christians. "But to make capital out of
them would only do more harm than good to the common cause
of evangelism and missions. . . . Moreover, disenchantment in the
national-missionary relationship is a two-way street. Along this
route one needs to look both ways. A careful appraisal of the relationship would show that the missionary is not wholly to blame
for the problems."[12]

This candid admission on the part of a national that the
"younger" churches do indeed fall short of perfection needs saying.[13] There has been a tendency to report in too glowing terms
the effects and results of turning over the church and mission
institutions to indigenous leadership. The results have mainly been
good. The withdrawal of a heavy missionary hand has permitted
able national leadership to come to the fore, often with a surge of
renewal in church life and expanded church growth, to say nothing of a sense of rootedness in native soil which freedom from
foreign control has given to the instruments of the Gospel in
their various forms. But there is another side of the coin, about
which missioners seldom write. Perhaps, motivated as we are so
strongly by the Western myth of success, we have had to see
this move of surrender on our part as successful too!

But all is not rosy in the younger churches, just as all is not rosy in the older churches which have sponsored the missions of which the younger churches are the fruit. Part of the yearning for the return of the missionary is a growing weariness with corruption in the leadership which in some instances followed his departure. Formerly animistic societies are peculiarly susceptible to the temptations of nepotism, a susceptibility related to the tribal structure of their societies. We expect a measure of nepotism in government, industry, and commerce, and there is an uncommon amount of it in Africa, as any observer of the African scene knows. But it is disappointing that the practice of appointing blood relatives to posts of leadership in the church, often without serious reference to their qualifications, and not infrequently at the expense of passing over better qualified applicants from a different family or clan, should be so marked a characteristic of church life in Africa, yet it is a fact.

And there is weariness with empty, repetitious sermons given by pastors or catechists more concerned with the size of their garden than their flock; more cognizant of the fluctuations in price of their coffee or cotton than the level of stewardship of their church members; more intent on petty commerce than preaching; often on the road, but seldom for reasons of evangelism. That these facts are related to the low level of remuneration characteristic of the ministry in these countries does not change the situation, even if we assign a fair share of the blame to the missionaries who left them with the system.

Particularly is there weariness with numerous instances of embezzlement of church funds at all levels which has only too frequently marked the transfer of authority from missionary to national. This is not to suggest that missionaries should return to resume the control of church treasuries. Often there has been no intent on the part of a church treasurer to make off with the money in his charge. He has rather yielded to enormous pres-

sures from a particular member or members of his clan for assistance in time of need, with the full intention of restoring the
funds to the treasury at a later date. But not a few church funds
have been depleted, some of them repeatedly, and this is a problem of prime magnitude for the young churches overseas.

The cry "Missionary, Come Back!" in this instance is a plea
for qualified missionary personnel to return to the service of the
church and teach it the 'how' of fiscal responsibility. Can we
truly ignore such a plea with the glib reply, "Let them learn
the hard way—Missionary, Stay Home!"?

I had a personal involvement in just such a problem on my
return to the Congo for re-immersion as a missionary. Functioning as physician in a mission hospital which had been transferred to church control in 1960, I was at the same time regarded as a counselor in evangelism and church polity by the
local church in the region. The regional church had been without
a missionary presence—indeed, virtually without supervision
from the particular branch of the national church involved—for
fully four years. During that time it had successively (but not
successfully) committed its treasury into the hands of an ordained pastor (the regional head of the church), and two schoolteachers, one of them the director of the regional primary
schools. Prior to the departure of missionaries during the 1964
rebellion, the treasurer had been for several years a national, a
chauffeur and trader by occupation, the missionaries having
played the role of counselors only. Each of the three treasurers
who functioned during the period after missionaries had departed misappropriated church funds. As a consequence, the pastors and catechists of the church had gone unpaid for many
months, although the particular regional church involved had
long had a reputation as having the highest sense of stewardship
of all the regional churches in that branch of the national church.

The leaders of the church, clerical and lay, came to me

quietly, and asked what they might do about the situation. Some in all seriousness asked that I exercise the authority of an apostle and call a general church meeting to settle the problem. This I was unwilling to do. But an occasion presented itself for a general meeting of all local and regional church officers when the vice-president of the Ubangi church came to visit the area for three weeks of evangelistic meetings. At the meeting which he called, the problem was aired and steps taken to introduce a system of checks and controls in which clerical and lay leadership would share, from the local through the district to the regional level. Noteworthy was the fact that there was no recrimination against those who had dipped their hands into the kitty. They were pardoned, and continue to enjoy positions of leadership both in the schools and church, though not as treasurers. This in itself is an index not only of the Africans' enormous long-sufferance and capacity for forgiveness, but a recognition of the relation of their peculiar problem to their own culture. It is also a clear indication that the white missionary had little to do with the decision!

What he could do however, and this is important to the context of our discussion, was to serve as a catalyst to precipitate a facing of a particular problem in the church; and to give the technical assistance that made a new start possible—in this instance, to suggest some better ways to handle church finances.

He could also re-introduce a dimension of charity and higher medical standards into the hospital, not by rule but by example. However we may be thrilled by the fact that the church has managed to keep medical institutions going with inadequately trained national personnel in the absence of missionary doctors, whatever pride we may feel in the accomplishments of African nurses who have performed life-saving surgery when no missionary surgeon remained to do the job, the fact remains that the level of medical care has fallen in many situations that have suffered the loss of missionary staff by reason of either revolution or devolution. Again it doesn't help simply to say, "It's our fault—we should have trained people faster to take our places," even though in most instances that may be true. Where we did train at high enough levels we did not always succeed in transmitting the same high sense of concern, the same degree of personal discipline, the same awareness of the value of good records and good accounting, the same love for the patient as a human being, and the same freedom from the temptations of a bribe that typical missionary doctors or nurses brought to their task. Medical care in mission hospitals now run by the church, or in some instances, by the state, simply is not as good as it used to be in a great many instances. Staff comes to work late, or misses without explanation. Stocks are not maintained, and in other instances are dissipated without being accounted for. Patients are neglected. And, because of the need for funds to pay staff, formerly furnished by the mission and/or state subsidy, rates are up and charity largely a thing of the past. There are notable exceptions to this description of a typical mission hospital now functioning without a missionary presence. But missionaries and visitors alike will recognize in this description a painfully accurate picture of many such situations.

It is no wonder that the people of regions once served by missionary staff in hospitals throughout the African bush are begging, "Missionary, Come Back!" Whether we respond affirmatively or not, whether indeed it would be well for us to respond, is not the immediate issue. I simply ask that we do not close our eyes and deny what we see.

One could say the same in the field of education. Enoc Sakofio, director of primary schools in the Karawa region of the Ubangi, responsible for some 8,000 pupils, on two occasions spent an hour with me making a plea for the return of a selected few missionaries to serve in the primary school system, which missionary staff left to the church to move "upward" into secondary school and university education after transfer. (Must we always move up? Can't we ever move sideways? Isn't part of the motivation for getting M.A.'s and Ph.D.'s the hidden desire to stay on top, and thus remain exactly in the same position we were in before transfer?) Mr. Sakofio pointed to the high failure-rate of students graduating from primary school, and the dearth of those who met entrance requirements for secondary school. He named two missionaries who had had a particular interest in and success with sixth grade pupils, and asked that they return, one to teach a special class of the most promising sixth graders he could cull from all the schools, the other to take those who almost but not quite made the entrance exams to secondary school and give them a post-primary, pre-secondary year of special tutoring. Educational missionary, come back!

It isn't merely that national primary school teachers have had an inadequate background in French and pedagogy (again, for reasons for which we share the blame). Too many are poorly motivated and simply do not care. I stopped at many a regional school during a tour of the Ubangi and found only too often that classrooms were already empty at eleven o'clock in the morning; the class already dismissed. In the case of pastors and nurses, a lack of concern could often be related to having received no pay for months, and be understandable. But teachers have been a favored lot in the Congo, and such indifference had deeper causes.

Not only in the institutional ministries of the church is there need and desire for missionaries. In Japan and the Congo (both within the past year) I heard a young church saying: "We want missionary evangelists, people who start churches and preach the Word of God." A Japanese pastor told me earnestly: "Into the rapidly developing suburbs of Tokyo we should be sending teams of two evangelists—a Japanese pastor and a missionary—working together to start new churches." The church he represented had recently moved into full autonomy, the mission having surrendered its charter to the church, and the missionaries in turn having been received into membership in the Japanese church. There was a notable spirit of oneness and hope, and the nationals were far from saying, "Missionary, Go Home!" They were saying, "Missionary, Stay!—and entice your younger brothers and friends to join us, too."[14]

Finally, the cry "Missionary, Come Back!" needs saying if only to offset the damage caused in the church in the homeland by too long playing of the other side of the record. There is little doubt that the constant reiteration of the theme "Missionary, Go Home!" in the pulpit and the press has had a serious effect on recruitment for desperately needed missionary replacements even in situations where no one was asking them to leave. Until very recently, when there have appeared some indices of change in the recruitment picture, hardly any gathering of mission executives escaped some sharing of mutual woe on the subject of the candidate gap.

It has also contributed to a drop of support for the missionary enterprise in general. Many of the major denominations have had to make serious cutbacks in their budgets for overseas mission, affecting not only staff but program, and jeopardizing their commitments to cooperative and ecumenical ventures. Even the "faith" boards and non-denominational missions have in some instances suffered curtailment of their ministries, and that in a time of unprecedented national prosperity. I am not trying to suggest a clear and exclusive cause-and-effect relationship between the constant repetition of the cry "Missionary, Go Home!" and these effects, but that it has contributed is hardly to be denied.

Missionaries have added to the din by saying, "I'm only there until I can work myself out of a job," conveying the impression, when they stay home for reasons of health, family, personal advantage, revolution, or disillusionment, that the task is indeed finished, when in reality it is not, or has simply changed character.

And they have suffered a loss of a sense of identity from hearing the cry "Missionary, Go Home!" Part of the current crisis in missionary role and image is surely in part at least the effect of this kind of sustained propaganda. Far from needing more of the same at the moment—most of the "wrong" kind of missionaries have already gone home—they need encouragement and help in redefining their role and mission. They will then be able and ready to reply affirmatively to the contrary cry, "Missionary, Come Back!," with joy and a new humility and dedication.[15]

Chapter 5

THE OTHER LEGACY

If there is another cry besides that of "Missionary, Go Home!," if there is indeed a plea "Missionary, Come Back!"—and we have seen that there is—it persists in part because there is another legacy besides the legacy of barriers which we described at the outset. The legacy of barriers is not the whole picture. Missionaries have not been all that bad, nor all that unpopular. Americans have not been all that ugly. If it is hard for a cynical Europe inured by repeated and long wars to recognize genuine idealism in American generosity, that does not mean that it was not there in the Marshall Plan, and in the flood of wheat and cattle that went from our shores to Europe at the close of World War II. When I studied French and tropical medicine on my way to the Congo in 1951–52 most Belgian acquaintances found it difficult to understand why a well-trained American doctor should want to leave his prosperous homeland to work at a low salary in the African bush. "Of course you'll have a chance to practice surgery on a lot of natives, and then you'll go back to the States to set up your own practice," they would finally conclude.

Again, if an Asia or Africa accustomed to bribery found it difficult to believe that behind the gift freely given there was not a lurking request for a later favor, it does not negate the fact that thousands of missionaries have been highly motivated with little thought of getting anything in return. This is not to say that their motives have not been mixed, nor that our own nation has been above economic imperialism! It is merely to insist that Americans as a people are uncommonly generous, and capable of much goodness, almost to the extent at times of being a stone of stumbling to the cynical world about them.

There is evidence that this characteristic of the American people is undergoing change, that we are becoming less generous and more cynical in our international relations. But even that does not alter history. And the cry "Missionary, Come Back!" is as much a product of goodness remembered as the cry "Missionary, Go Home!" was a product of evil remembered.

For there *is* another legacy. It is the *legacy of bridges* built by the faithful witness and service of hundreds of missionaries over scores of years in multiple human situations, flashes of the true ministry of reconciliation known to the missionary by his awareness of God's grace to him—reflected in remembered acts which help to nullify the other dark legacy of which we have written.

This legacy too has its scenes: the white missionary nurse getting up night after night at the beckoning of the African sentry to help a frightened and exhausted Congolese mother bring her child to birth, or to save one born in a squalid hut and now bent in the painful opisthotonus of tetanus, or to sponge the hot body of a malarial child with tender alcoholic wipings . . . the missionary teacher sitting in the back of the jouncing truck on the metallic hardness of a gasoline drum for a full day's journey in the sun and rain, so that the pastor's wife with her newborn infant might sit in the cab in front . . . the missionary evangelist removing his coat in the cool of the night to wrap the shivering child sitting beside him in the back of the truck . . . the busy doctor stopping at the village simply to chat with the old chief on whom he had once operated for an incarcerated hernia, to ask him about his wives and children and how he fares.

This legacy of bridges is one of understanding, mutuality, communion, and love, of hope and common concerns, bridges of shared suffering and danger, worship and prayer, sickness and tears, imprisonment and death. It is the memory of shared meals in missionary and African homes, of shared laughter, of the shared excitement of the hunt, of the sharing at the Lord's table, and the prayer conference where African and white roomed together. It is volleyball games and the beating of bricks and singing carols and bathing in cool streams and riding in the back of trucks together. It is the silent sitting that marks an African wake, the confrontation and sharing of mourning together with the sacrament of mere human presence, and the common death of a Paul Carlson and an Ambroise Kokembe from rebel bullets.

Even the colonial legacy deserves a second look. We are now far enough removed historically from the events out of which emerged a host of newly independent nations in Asia and Africa, chiefly after World War II, to take such a look. L. H. Gann and Peter Duignan have dared to swim against the current and do just that in a bold reappraisal of the colonial legacy in a volume done under the auspices of the Hoover Institute and entitled *Burden of Empire.* The book is a careful re-evaluation of the plusses and minuses of European imperialism on the continent of Africa. They conclude Chapter Twenty-two, "Imperial Balance Sheet: A Summing Up," with these words:

> The imperialists can plead that, even within their critics' own unspoken terms of reference, the colonial record involved tremendous achievements for good as well as ill. In our view, the imperial system stands out as one of the most powerful engines for cultural diffusion in the history of Africa; its credit balance by far outweighs its debit account.[1]

One is likely to react: "Powerful engines indeed! But what do engines care about people?" And the reaction itself suggests how deeply we are ourselves caught in certain presuppositions, girded by a new romanticism that marks our era, which suffers, like all romanticisms, from an inherent incapacity for objectivity.

Let us look at the other legacy of colonialism, then, through the eyes of Gann and Duignan, if only to prove to ourselves that we have not closed our own. Having penned the lines of my first two chapters above, it is no small exercise for me personally!

To begin with it should be noted that the authors of *Burden of Empire* by no means gloss over the negative aspects of the European occupation of the African continent. They give this side its full due. Their concern is to set the record straight, and especially to counteract several current interpretations of African history which they find to be sheer romanticism, and, as such, as unrealistic as the "old-fashioned, flag-waving, sentimental Edwardian view of history!"

They remind us, refreshingly, I think, that the moral revulsion against *all* empire which characterizes modern man is a recent phenomenon. From the beginning of recorded history until recent times man has gloried in the splendor of empire. True, the prophets have railed against the strong who abused their power to the hurt of the weak, but biblical writers have generally joined those of other cultures in praising the kings who extended the borders of their own people. This modern revulsion against empire "had its origins in the West, where it went hand in hand with a reaction against any kind of authority, moral, religious, political, or economic, which did not rest—or which elaborate and specious manipulation did not make appear to rest —on the free consent of the governed."[2]

Marxist views of economics and Freudian views of personality combined to effect the re-evaluation of empire, so that hidden motives were found in the minds of the mighty, and Western imperialism in Africa became a Satanic thing, motivated neither by the glory of expansion nor the extension of civilization, but by money. Colonial exploitation, it was argued, drained Africa of its riches, and left the West with a great moral and economic debt to the African peoples, who should now be compensated for "a century of wrong." Thus argue a majority of educated Africans today, and they are joined by a host of Western thinkers, who, the writers suggest, feel "a secularized sense of guilt" for the wrongs done by whites in Africa.

Gann and Duignan take exception to the view which sees European expansion in Africa as a huge money game. There is no justification, they state, "for the romantic theory that the true imperial decisions were made by the Rothschilds and the Bleichroders from the obscurity of a countinghouse."[3] The scramble for Africa at the end of the nineteenth century must be seen in a much larger context, as part of a much longer story of imperial conquest, only superficially related to an abundance of capital seeking investment opportunities overseas. Imperialism was highly pluralistic in motivation, concerned not only with money, but trade and real estate, relief of national border pressures in Europe, religion and idealism, national prestige and glory. And in a profound sense, it was the result of Africa's own weakness. This is not to deny the black man's pre-colonial achievements, a subject strongly stressed (and rightly so) in current literature. It is simply to deny that European imperialism or even the slave trade *caused* Africa's backwardness.

The so-called Christian slave trade had rested on an Afro-European partnership in which powerful African potentates sold their prisoners to the white men from beyond the seas. Why then did Africans sell their captives? Because they wanted European trade goods—cloth, guns, knives, hatchets, liquor, and beads. Backward African economies could not produce some of these items at all or in sufficient quantities, or they could not buy them in the desired quantities by means of "legitimate" trade. African rulers were therefore unable on their own to cope with the problems of the slave trade, Christian or Muslim. Abolition came from without, and only European suzerainty could, for the time being, repair the ravages of the gun frontier that was converging on the African interior during the last century.[4]

The guns themselves illustrate the problem. Guns, the authors continue,

were themselves the products of a highly complex industrial, technical, and scientific culture, which African tribesmen might envy but could not at the time imitate. The white man was also more advanced in the field of ideas. The production even of machine guns required ideological foundations much broader than those possessed by any contemporary African society. The white man's most important contribution to Africa did not consist of arms or even of quinine tablets. His most important imports were perhaps the very words Africa and African.[5]

There was, of course, no sense of unity among the peoples of pre-colonial Africa, who thought of themselves as members of particular tribes. European colonial rule was a liberating as well as a restricting force, doing away not only with the slave trade, but also with the restraints on ordinary trade and production which indigenous authorities imposed. Although it introduced segregation between white and black—the evil of which the authors recognize—it did away with indigenous caste differentiation. Furthermore, although the white man won advantages for himself in occupying Africa, the black often shared in the same advantages, and many Africans preferred the new order to the old.

> The people who had actual experience of precolonial Africa, of local despotism, of the social and economic limitations which beset contemporary African kingdoms, of their intellectual narrowness, their rigid social stratification, their poverty, witchcraft executions, political mass liquidations, the superstitious destruction of twins as harbingers of evil, or intertribal warfare—these people did not regard preconquest Africa in the same light as so many modern scholars, whose work is all too often infused both by a nagging sense of guilt and by a generous but deceptive romanticism concerning the glories of a departed society.[6]

The argument that, left alone, pre-colonial tribal Africa would have coalesced into larger states and developed into advanced industrial societies rivaling those of Europe gets little support from a study of the experience of, say, Ethiopia, which, except for a brief period of Italian occupation, was free to profit from nearly uninterrupted self-determination. Ethiopia possessed a written language, considerable military and cultural resources, and a large land area endowed with notable natural resources. Yet its achievements in comparison with other African states that experienced colonial occupation bring it up short, and leave little ground for optimism "concerning the assumed capacity for more effective African development on an indigenous basis during the imperial era."[7] A similar case could be made were Liberia to be chosen as an example, or Haiti, or Afghanistan, which are among the most poverty-stricken nations on earth.

Because the Belgians have been perhaps the most maligned of

the colonial powers for their record in their colony, the Congo, and because that is the area of my own acquaintance, it may be instructive to re-examine that record. The Belgians took command of a country whose people had attained the technology of the Early Iron Age, whose foreign trade was largely confined to the export of slaves, ivory, and some copper. In a relatively short time they made it one of the greatest copper producers in the world and the world's leading exporter of cobalt. They built rails, port facilities, workshops, power plants, waterworks, and cement factories, housing projects, public utilities and services, and expanded roads and water transport. In fact, the mining industry acted as a great "multiplier-accelerator" of economic growth, so that towns multiplied, trade increased, goods became universally available, and farming enterprises were stimulated. By the end of 1950 the Belgian Congo was the second ranking power producer of hydroelectricity on the African continent. The rapid expansion of secondary industries was such that few countries ever attained a faster rate of industrial growth. "The mines and factories, the railways and ports, put up under Belgian management represented a truly creative achievement, the result of the colonizer's own enterprise capital and skills."[8]

But what of the people of the land, the Congolese themselves? And wasn't the price too high, with the Belgians reaping exorbitant profits? According to Hailey, in 1953, fifty-six per cent of the national income was received by Africans, fourteen per cent entered the coffers of the companies.[9] Martelli calculates that the annual average return of Belgian capital on an investment of about one billion pounds yielded no more than four to five per cent over the years, comparable to what could have been secured in Europe, and that practically every man-made thing of capital value in the Congo today was left there by the Belgians.[10] "Taking colonial development as a whole, it is nonsense to say that the imperialists joined in plundering Africa. The dramatic increases from production in most colonies benefited all concerned, the peasant producers and the workers as well as expatriate interests."[11]

The Belgians also gave the Congo one of the highest literacy rates among the underdeveloped countries of the world. Although in higher education they did less well (deliberately, no doubt) they did better than critics have credited them. The oft-quoted figure of "sixteen university graduates" left to the Congo when it became independent ignores the fact that the number of persons with the equivalent of an average American college education—the *diplomés*—was about 4,000, and that because of its solid primary school base the Congo is actually better equipped to succeed as a nation than those newly independent countries with an excess (in relation to their stage of development) of educated élite trained in Europe or America.

Critics of Western imperial rule forget that no other empires have been judged by their capacity for self-liquidation, nor are contemporary Communist empires so judged (though reaction to Russia's reoccupation of Czechoslovakia suggests that this is changing). The fact is that colonial empire in Africa transferred vast human and physical capital *to* Africa, more perhaps than was ever withdrawn, not the least of which were the efforts of privately subsidized mission societies which alone, in the opinion of Gann and Duignan, "form an outstanding chapter in the history of civilization."[12]

The West brought a host of new economic, medical, social, and administrative techniques to Africa which played a decisive role in its history. If Africa today glories in a past which it is rediscovering, it owes that rediscovery to the white rulers of the continent whose documentation of their occupation constitutes the only written record available, and whose archeologists and anthropologists have done—and continue to do—the research which has unearthed the facts in which Africans may glory.

Actually the colonial occupation was an exceedingly brief one, measured in historic perspective, and this makes its achievements all the more spectacular. Moreover, with the exception of the blot of the slave trade which colonial occupation itself brought to an end, bloodshed was minimal, and the mass liquidations and expulsions involving millions of people which marked the rule of totalitarian governments in Central and Eastern Europe as well as Asia, were not paralleled in Africa.[13] The continent was largely sheltered from major war (though the French used large numbers of African troops abroad); it got administrative stability, and freedom from corruption in government; government was limited rather than total, so that much real freedom remained. And when final freedom was granted, it got its impetus from the very capacity of the imperial West for self-criticism, unique in history. Thus the modern African critic of empire derives his thesis not from African, but Western roots. He is indebted to those he criticizes for the very vocabulary he uses, with words like "freedom" and "self-determination," and he writes in the language of the very imperial power that gave him his education.

When he charges the colonial entrepreneur with exploitation, he does not bother to compare the wages paid black workmen by black employers, which are usually substantially less than those paid by white employers; nor is he likely to admit that the living standards of laborers for European companies are vastly superior to those of other laborers, and rapidly improving.

The former colonialist cannot win for losing. If he invests money in African enterprises, he is guilty of taking profit out of the country. If he does not, he is neglecting a former dependency and showing bad blood! If a Western capitalist lends money to an African state, he is guilty of indirect exploitation. If he refuses a loan, he is boycotting the development of the new nations!

The colonial occupation of Africa actually seized relatively small amounts of land. (Compare the treatment of the American Indian, for example). And the value of what was seized has greatly appreciated under European management, through new farming methods and technology, leaving an improved legacy of benefit to Africans as well as Europeans. That in some areas this worked to the deprivation of indigenous peoples is not denied, but the balance sheet is not on the side of those who claim exploitation.

And exploitation has been a two-way street. The metropolitan governments often gave imperial preference to their colonies. Thus Frenchmen pay more for Senegalese peanuts and Italians more for Somali bananas than the world prices call for. (Just as Americans used to pay more for Cuban sugar.)

Finally, a look at what has happened to the nations which achieved independence at the price of a rapid or precipitous withdrawal of Europeans in large numbers should convince even the blind that the European presence was hardly a completely negative quantity. If we exclude Guinea from consideration (because there the French left in spite and were actually destructive in departure), what is the general picture? The Congo, Nigeria, Algeria—all have suffered a huge loss in skills and purchasing power, order and employment, peace and standard of living.

This is not to wish the return of the colonialist, or to whitewash the negative aspects of the imperialist occupation. It is merely to set the record straight, and to ask for perspective. There is small danger that the person who responds to the call "Missionary, Come Back!" today will come imbued with pride. The West today is closer to depression than delusions of grandeur. It is rather to suggest that he go free of guilt, which can only hinder effective communication. There is also little danger that he be received with anything akin to worship! But it will help neither Africa nor the West to receive him as an agent of exploitation. If he is willing to go as a brother, he deserves to be received as one.

We may argue with Gann and Duignan, whose argument is essentially an economic as opposed to an idealist one. And we risk censure by African and liberal friends for including it in a volume on Christian mission. But African leadership itself appreciates the Western legacy more than diatribes meant to prove its African neo-nationalism normally convey. Tributes to the colonial West are not lacking in African speeches. We mentioned in Chapter 4 having heard speeches by President Joseph D. Mobutu lauding the work of Christian missionaries, both Catholic and Protestant, over the national radio of the Democratic Republic of the Congo (Kinshasa); and of similar sentiments expressed on the occasion of the dedication of the Paul Carlson Evangelical Medical Center, by the Minister of Agriculture, Mr. Litho, who represented the central government at the ceremony, as well as by Mr. Jonas Mukamba, the governor of the Equator province.

Nor are such tributes lacking in African writings. The missionary journal *Africa Now* recently carried a reprint of an editorial from the *Daily Telegraph*, a Nigerian newspaper in Lagos with a reputation for nationalism, which takes to task a Mr. Udemezuo Onyido who had written an article in the same paper the day before strongly critical of the work of Christian missionaries. The editor defends missionaries of the charge of having wreaked havoc in Africa in their attempt to Christianize the continent, of having destroyed, according to Mr. Onyido, the culture, the music, and the religion of Africans. Taking issue with this charge in considerable detail, he goes on to credit missionaries with not only having done a good job in Africa, but also with having saved Africa through the introduction of Christianity.

He cites as evidence the fact that most of the schools and colleges in Nigeria were built and financed by missionaries, and that the same must be said for most of Nigeria's hospitals, maternity centers, dispensaries, and leprosaria. He states that most African leaders received their education in mission schools, and that Mr. Onyido himself had. He argues that those elements in African culture which fell to the onslaught of the Christian gospel deserved to die. Christianity, he declares, taught Africans the meaning of love, and the missionaries who brought this message are deserving of praise.[14]

And whether said by Africans or not, indeed, whether said by the sons of the colonizers or not, there remains a legacy only now coming to be appreciated, even at the place of origin, in which Africans and Europeans, including Americans, share. I refer to the fact of secularization, a subject to which we will give greater attention in Chapter Seven, but which we should introduce here, since it may well be one of the most significant of the legacies that the Christian missionary movement and Western colonialism together gave to the third world.

There is a hint of this in *Burden of Empire*, where it is suggested that the profound economic, political, and social changes which the imperial occupation of Africa produced would not have been possible apart from that occupation, because those changes were grounded in fundamental ideological, or more exactly, ideational differences between Africa and the West. The root of those differences is the Christian faith, which, however poorly it may be understood and practiced in the West itself, nonetheless is the only factor distinctive to the West capable of accounting for the difference.[15]

Secularization, as Dr. van Leeuwen defines it, is the emancipation of man from religious constraints, or as Newbigin puts it, "the withdrawal of more and more areas of human experience from direct reference to religion."[16] Paradoxically, it has its origins in religion—specifically the religion of Israel. It was Israel who broke with the Greek conception of the cosmos, which saw

the world in exclusively spatial terms, as well as with the ontocratic religions of the Near East, whose mythical view of the
world entrapped man in the everlasting cycle of nature. For in
the great cultures and religions of the past, the temporal and
the eternal, the human and the divine were united in sacralized
social structures, whose orders possessed divine authority and
were therefore unchallengeable.

The impact of the Gospel on the world has been to shatter
the whole ontocratic pattern and desacralize all spheres of historical existence. Israel had seen that human existence is determined by the dimension of time and history, for the Covenant
between the Creator and his chosen People had burst the solidarity of the universe and made man free. But it took the Gospel
to free this view of the world and man's life in it from the ethnic
confines in which its identification with Israel had held it.

Curiously—perhaps predictably—as the ancient religions of
man retreat before the Gospel and the world becomes Chris-
tianized and freed from domination by pagan sacral powers, the
church herself is tempted to domination as a religion bearing the
label Christian.

But, Dr. van Leeuwen continues, the Word of God is
"sharper than any two-edged sword" (Heb. 4:12 KJV), and
"judgment begins with the household of God" (I Peter 4:17
RSV, paraphrased); Christianity, now a world religion, becomes
responsible for secularization, as the creative and liberating activity of the Word of God stirs new forces into active life. The
very world she frees protests the church's own domination,
lending voice to the Word the church herself proclaims half-
understandingly. The consequence for man is a new freedom.
Liberated from all external authority structures, both the individual and the community are freed to respond to new possibilities of fulfillment and to shape their future as they wish.
Newbigin aptly describes the change:

In the old type of village community men are confined to
the society of their neighbors and they have no choice of
friends. In a modern city, aided by a car or telephone, a
man can ignore his neighbors and choose his friends at will.
He is thus free, in large measure, to choose the standards
under which he will live. Nothing is, in quite the old sense,
given. The same freedom extends to other areas of life.
The form of government under which he will live . . . the
way in which one earns one's living . . . money . . . less and
less is mankind compelled to accept the facts of social, political, and economic life as given: more and more are they
matters for deliberate decision.[17]

The point for this discussion is that the new freedom with
its new possibilities would not have emerged on the basis of the
ancient religions of Asia, or of African animism. They presup-
pose in effect the Christian Gospel of creation, redemption, and
resurrection, the faithful proclamation of which throughout the
world by Christian missionaries has been uniformly followed not
only by the birth of a church but by secularization. An ontocratic society resists change, for the patterns of existence have become sacralized. The Gospel—and the societies which have become identified with it—proclaims the possibility, indeed, the
necessity of change, and it is this attitude which has led the West
to a rapidly accelerating control of the forces of nature and life.
Wesley Nelson describes this with particular clarity:

Change is the chief difference between our time and the
past, and it is the presence of change that characterizes
this as a secular age. It is not just that we are able to exercise so much more control over the forces around us
that produces the secular attitude; it is that we are making
such great progress in assuming control of these forces.
The rapidly expanding secular attitude of our day is due

largely to the rapidly accelerating rate of change which makes it normal for man to think of eventually controlling his environment. Therefore, though the basic elements of secularity are not new, the additional element of rapidly accelerating change which characterizes our day is what makes this a uniquely secular age.[18]

If Africans today look to a new Africa, moving to a better future while reflecting African values, they largely owe the look itself to the entry of Europeans, however mixed their record, into their continent. More particularly, they owe it to those among them who bore the Good News of Christ.

Chapter 6

_____

THE RECOVERY OF SENT-NESS

Much of the debate between "Missionary, Go Home!" and "Missionary, Come Back!" misses a very central point. There is a sense, in fact, in which the whole discussion is academic. Has God withdrawn His mandate? Is Jesus no longer saying "Go therefore, and make disciples of all nations" (Matt. 28:19 RSV) as he said to his apostles? The Great Commission has been the primary motivation of missionaries through the centuries of expansion of the Christian Church. Is even that passé?

The very word missionary implies that one is sent, even as the word mission implies a sending. Derived from the Latin, *mitto*, "I send," both words indicate the response of the believing Christian and a faithful church to Jesus Christ, the Lord, the One who sends. Ultimately it is beside the point whether the missionary receives his orders from the mission or the church, or from an older or younger church, or from a Western or Eastern one, a European, American, Asian, Latin, or African one. It is Jesus Christ who commands, and under whose orders he serves. The missionary may indeed sometimes have to oppose the orders of both the church at home and the church abroad to be faithful to the command of Christ.

I well remember a meeting of all the ordained men in the Evangelical Church of the Ubangi, called for reasons of spiritual fellowship and prayer around the Word of God, shortly after a tense annual meeting during which transfer of authority from mission to church was made, just after independence came to the former Belgian Congo in 1960. There had been a measure of hurt at that meeting, which had strongly polarized missionary and national leadership, and we needed to get together to let the balm of the Holy Spirit heal our wounds. It was a fully integrated meeting, with rooms and meals shared as well as the prayer and Bible-study sessions. I gave one of the studies, and chose to make the point that neither the mission in the past, nor the church now, ultimately had the authority to say whether or not a man could preach. I said to my Congolese brethren:

> It is possible that you may not ask us to preach, now that yours is the responsibility to assign the men to the preaching missions. And if you don't I for one shall remain silent for a time. But after awhile I shall break that silence, whether you invite me to or not. For our call is not finally from you nor the sending church in our homeland. It comes from the Lord Himself. There are yet villages here that have not heard the Gospel, and God has not rescinded our call with transfer.

That little speech was well received by our Congolese brethren, I should add.

I am not suggesting a return to anarchic individualism. No one can spend a decade and more in central Africa without coming to some appreciation of the meaning of community! Nor am I ignoring the mystery of the laying on of hands in ordination, nor the significance of the consecration of missionaries by the body of those who constitute an annual meeting of the church or other group that sets a missionary aside for his task, sending him out with a community of support. Nor am I opposing change. Change in method is sorely needed, even if our motive remains unchanging. The new wine of the Gospel breaks not only the vessels that receive it, but the skins out of which it is poured. I am simply trying to recover an element that is often lost in the heat of debate on the place of the foreign missionary in today's world.

That element used to be summed up in the word "call." One was "called" to be a missionary, and sent because he was called. This was true whether one went out under a denominational board or "faith" board. We do not speak so confidently about a call today.

There are many reasons. A few people, by any standard of measurement, were obviously *not* called of God. They went of their own volition or under pressures from others, and where they went, they did more harm than good. They became barriers to the Gospel's reception, rather than instruments of it. By their performance, or lack of it, they brought disrepute to the calling. Others did well enough in the "field," or at least were harmless there, but communicated poorly at home, so that they cast doubt on the validity of their call. Even very able missionaries—able in field work—sometimes communicate poorly on itineration and as a consequence contribute to such doubts.

This is in part due to the persistence of the missionary myth, a kind of image or body of beliefs about missionaries still prominent in fundamentalist circles to a degree and present even in the mainline denominations. That the myth persists is surprising, since missionary communication has improved a great deal in the past decade. This myth perpetuates either the classic picture of the Bible-toting (King James, of course) somber and joyless person dressed in out-of-style clothing who goes to a "savage" tribe, and there presents a Jonathan Edwards version of the Gospel; or his twentieth-century successor, a "skilled missionary flying his plane, resolving his linguistic problems, operating his jungle radio, shooting rapids on his raft, bidding his lovely wife and kiddies good-bye—and always with that heroic sense of purpose and sacrifice,"[1] still, may I add, faithfully presenting the Edwardian gospel. Dave Christensen, a senior medical student from Temple University, gives his reaction to a short-term missionary experience in these terms:

> I found conditions better than I expected. . . . It is human to generate sympathy and support by emphasizing unpleasant conditions and hardships. . . . I was under the impression that one Mission hospital was difficult, discouraging. . . . I pictured the doctor there to be skinny with bags under his eyes from lack of sleep. . . . There is the general consensus in the homeland that missionaries are living martyrs.[2]

Mr. Christensen found running water, electricity, peace and quiet, and time to read. The point is that an intelligent young man growing up in a representative American Protestant church had absorbed a false image of missionaries from his limited contacts with them and the church's literature on overseas mission. This particular young man was not as a consequence disillusioned. But others have been, and the effect is to cast doubt upon the missionary call.

Again, the American culture is a success culture, and the hard fact is that few missionaries today are bounding home with 'success'. On the contrary, most are finding out that their role is no longer to be a big frog in a little pond, but a little frog in a big pond; that they are called to be servants, vulnerable, insecure, often unhearkened to, even rejected at times, as was their Lord.

The transition to such a role is not an easy one, and many missionaries find themselves unable to make it. Used to describ-

ing their activities in terms of a successful operation replete with
impressive statistics—so many souls saved, so many in attendance
at a youth camp, so many patients treated at a dispensary, so
many pupils enrolled in primary school, so many pieces of literature distributed, so many listeners' letters in response to a radio
program—they are uncomfortable in their new role, which is
less conducive to securing a generous response at home from a
church accustomed to measure the success of anything in statistical terms. And some feel constrained to wonder if, unable to
produce statistics that suggest success, they were indeed called of
God after all.

Americans suffer too from the need to be popular. It is an
almost pathological need in our society; so much so that when it
is denied us we tread on the margins of paranoia. It is not without significance that the title of Bishop Dodge's book should be
The UNPOPULAR Missionary. I doubt that that was the
Bishop's own title—his publisher had an eye on the market!
But it says something about our national character. It is certainly normal to want to be liked, but with Americans the desire to be liked borders on an obsession. It marks our church
life as well. And it is small wonder that missionaries produced in
American churches should share this trait.

That Americans suffer from anti-American propaganda is
obvious. Part of the difficulty in getting foreign aid bills through
the Congress arises from a reaction to the graffiti and broken embassy windows and burnt flags, as well as to the torrent of anti-
Americanism in the foreign press. Our generosity seems unappre-
ciated, and it hurts. Missionaries share in the sense of hurtness.
And it is easy to move from there into the dangerous area of self-
pity, from which it is a short step to a serious questioning of
one's call. In the long line of biblical prophets one can readily
find companions!

But there is something deeper than a susceptibility to wounds

from mere unpopularity. One wonders if there is not some substance to the charge that Americans are going soft. Is it indeed
possible to grow increasingly affluent without getting soft? The
history of nations suggests that it probably is not. Is not part of
the loss of call to uncomfortable places traceable to the fact that
we like comfort? Are there not missionaries who are secretly
(or otherwise) happy to hear the cry "Missionary, Go Home!"
because they are sick and tired of being shoved around, repeatedly evacuated, or given uninspiring assignments by an un-
imaginative indigenous leadership that has yet to discover the best
way to use the missionary's gifts?

Perhaps we need to reread our New Testament. Certainly
our Lord did not promise his disciples an easy life: "Behold, I
send you forth as sheep in the midst of wolves" (Matt. 10:16
KJV). He suggested that persecution would be a normal part of
life, that in fact, we should beware when all men speak well of
us: "Woe to you, when all men speak well of you, for so their
fathers did to the false prophets" (Luke 6:26 RSV). He told his
followers not to go before kings with prepared speeches—the
Holy Spirit would give them words to speak (Matt. 10:19–20).
All these passages suggest a kind of existential naïveté in the face
of hardship. If the world is today saying "Missionary, Go
Home!" is it not possible that this is the very moment when
we should be most faithful to our call, and at the very places
from which the cry emanates?

Obviously, we must be careful here. Jesus also enunciated
the dust principle, counseling his disciples that there is a time and
there are places to leave when one is unwanted (Luke 10:10–12).
But in the eschatological context of that counsel it is obvious
that the dust principle is not related so much to the fact of not
being well received or wanted as to the question of priorities
and the judicious use of limited time and resources.

And we must not be guilty of fostering any martyr complexes either. This is hardly a serious danger, if the precipitous evacuation of the missionary force from the Congo following the events of independence in 1960 is any index. On that occasion there were few seekers after martyrdom. There was an almost unseemly haste about departure, and a grasping for rumor that suggested a lack of dedication in the traditional missionary sense, particularly on the part of males. (And we haven't time here to speculate on what may well be another factor in the loss in American Christianity of a sense of call—the demasculinization of the American male!)

With these acknowledged cautions, is it not possible that the stubborn return of missionaries to a hostile environment, shorn of the past familiar securities of various power structures, whether church or state, military or civil, intellectual or technological, may force a second look at the message they bring by those to whom they bring it?

I sensed something of this during our recent stay in the Congo—a kind of grudging admiration for those missionaries who kept returning in spite of repeated turmoil, because this was their call. They had acquired a kind of apostolic status, personally earned, unrelated to their sending body or nationality. Enough Congolese have now traveled abroad to know how Americans live at home, and to wonder from a different point of view at the persistent return of their missionary friends to a place where they live less well, have poorer facilities for their children's education, suffer from exotic diseases non-existent in their homeland, and take orders from people with far less education than themselves. These missionaries have acquired acceptance and their quiet voices are heard. And this acceptance is based not so much on the particular talents they bring, or the money their work attracts from abroad, or the sense of relatedness to a larger world their presence symbolizes, but from a recognition that they are truly sent of God, and cannot deny their mission in spite of whatever personal advantages such denial might bring them.

It is time to recover the sense of Sent-ness, to appreciate again the mystery of the missionary call. I do not mean a sharpening of the universal dichotomy of priest and parishioner, of clergy and layman, nor of the peculiarly Western schizogeny of the religious and secular, as subsequent chapters will clearly show. I mean quite simply the recovery of the sense, on the part of those who go, that they are sent, and that they are impelled to go by the Holy Spirit. A lay missionary in secular employment, a short-term technician, and a career missionary can share equally in this conviction.

We cannot leave this discussion without facing the issue of universalism. It can hardly be doubted that the widespread and growing acceptance of this doctrine (or heresy, as the case may be) has contributed most significantly to a dampening of missionary motivation. The thousands of missionaries who streamed out during the great missionary era now past to what were then the far corners of the earth were convinced of the desperate need of the masses to whom they went to hear the Gospel. Indeed, they were convinced that without the Gospel, men were irrevocably lost.

Their era coincided with a kind of preaching in which people heard about heaven and hell. Most people today rarely, if ever, hear such sermons, and most young people in our churches have grown up without the traditional sense of the world's lostness. Tolerance replaced confrontation (although recently confrontation, on new and different issues, seems again to have replaced tolerance). A God of love (until He recently died at the hands of theologians) replaced the terrible God of judgment. Often what passed for tolerance was mere ignorance or indifference. But that hardly changes the fact. And as a consequence of the change, the obvious happened: It became boorish to proselytize on behalf of Christianity. Those engaged in the business began to feel ill at ease. Christianity became just one of several religions, one road of many leading to heaven (whatever that might be), and hardly the best macadam at that.

There was need for a corrective to a Gospel whose claim to uniqueness had come to be too closely associated with a particular cultural expression, that of the Christian West. To the extent that it provides such corrective, universalism bears a hearing. The Bible itself anticipates the need, for the tenets of universalism do not lack their proof-texts in the Scripture any more than does a doctrine of hell, or an insistence that Christ alone offers salvation. But to offer a corrective is one thing. To become an executioner is another. And the wide acceptance of the belief in the ultimate salvation of all men leaves a large segment of would-be missioners without adequate motivation for their going.

The triune God, whom Christians worship as Father, Son, and Holy Spirit, is indeed the God of all men. He is not the exclusive possession of those whose knowledge of him, in addition to what was perceptible in nature and deducible from history, has come from faith in Jesus Christ, in whom He revealed Himself supremely, and, in a sense, finally. God does not deny His love to those who through ignorance or error, or lack of opportunity to hear the truth, do not worship Him in truth. The rain falls on them, the sun shines on them, even as on the more knowledgeable believer (Matt. 5:45). Light in a measure shines for them, too, even if they have not yet seen "the true Light, which lighteth every man that cometh into the world" (John 1:9 KJV). And cosmic chlorophyll is not wholly lacking in the chemistry of their spirit, for in many who are not Christian "the fruits of the Spirit" appear—"love, joy, peace, patience, kindness, goodness, faithfulness, gentleness, self-control" (Gal. 5:22–23 RSV)—surely the response to such light as gets through.

The universalist insists that our part as Christians in God's mission is to help men to open their eyes wider, that they may see the Christ who is their Savior. We are not sent nor do we go to bring Christ to the nations. He is already there. The call to missionary witness comes from the Christ who dwells among them, and who is there long before we ever arrive with the Good News of His coming. As one writer puts it:

> The Triune God is there long before we arrive. Strange as it may seem, he does not complete his work there except through the Christian mission. The task of that mission is to show to his people, with whom he already dwells, the nature of that divine Presence. Thus they are enabled to perform that act of accepting the Christ, who is already theirs, as their Lord and Savior. This is the act essential to salvation.[3]

The difficulty lies in the fact that this kind of strangeness, this sense that God does not complete His work except through Christian witness, is not so impelling a force for witness as was the earlier picture of a lost and sinful world bound for an everlasting hell. Somehow, the task seems less urgent, and our part in it less necessary, if Christ, who alone is the Savior, is already among them and waits only for the scales to fall from their eyes.

Perhaps this is the case because of our pride. There was something great about God needing us so desperately to accomplish His purposes. And perhaps our rejection of universalism is in part a very human rejection of this affront—this telling us that we weren't really needed that badly to save the world after all.

But more than our pride is offended. So is that most precious of God's gifts to man—human freedom. And many of us so cherish that gift that we must insist before God Himself that man remain ever free to love or reject Him. It is on this count particularly that I find universalism wanting. For if all men are indeed to be saved, freedom is a farce. It matters little whether God overwhelms us with will or with love. To find the choice ultimately rigged would be to discover that love itself is hell, a discovery many a child smothered in mother-love has made, often to his own bitterness and his mother's sorrow. The love of God is not coercively possessive, nor is it Himself He loves. "For God so loved the *world*, that he *gave* . . . (John 3:16 KJV). And a gift is something to be accepted or rejected. Where there is no possibility of rejection the gift reduces either to a payment or a bribe and it is inconceivable that God by His very nature should make either. Harold Lindsell summarizes the position of conservative evangelicals in the following:

> Universalism is an impossibility precisely because of man's freedom. To suppose that all men would freely and of their own choice lay hold of Jesus Christ for salvation and the forgiveness of sins is patently foolish. . . . Universalism could only mean that God sovereignly forces all men to faith in Jesus Christ. For him so to act would be to deny man the power of contrary choice and to make untrue the biblical account of the introduction of sin. But more than this, it would make almost a monster of God, for if he sovereignly brings all men to eternal life, he should then in sovereignty have prevented man from sinning in the first place. To allow . . . men and nations to act as they have acted across the centuries is to make God not only the redeemer but the originator, the author of sin. To deal with this problem by suggesting that the entrance of sin came by human act and decision but that the restoration of all things comes by sovereign fiat (which it must if there is universalism) is as irrational as it is unbiblical.[4]

The conservative evangelical so writes because he believes

that the mission of the church takes as its point of departure a fact which is at once historic and existential—the conviction that something is fundamentally wrong with man, that he is, in short, a sinner, and by reason of his sin estranged from God. "All have sinned and fall short of the glory of God" (Rom. 3:23 RSV). "None is righteous, no not one" (Rom. 3:10 RSV). "All we like sheep have gone astray; we have turned everyone to his own way" (Isa. 53:6 KJV). He understands salvation as salvation from sin, and finds in the death of Jesus, on the cross, the act by which atonement for sin is made and salvation made possible. And he insists with the writer of Acts that "there is salvation in no one else, for there is no other name under heaven given among men by which we must be saved" (Acts 4:12 RSV).

That a conviction that this is the way it is in God's design is potent motivation for missionary service is evidenced by the fact that during the past four decades the smaller and more conservative denominations together with the independent faith boards have increased their personnel far out of proportion to the numbers sent by major denominations. At the annual meeting of the Division of Overseas Ministries of the National Council of Churches held in New Haven, Connecticut, November 19–22, 1968, David Stowe made the same point. Less than forty per cent of the overseas missionary force is now related to churches in the National Council of Churches of America.[5] It is difficult to escape the conviction that the traditional motivation of the conservative groups is a more potent force than that moving the churches where this has been diluted by universalism.

But to conclude therefrom that the answer to renewal in mission, the clue to a recovery of Sent-ness, is simply to turn back the clock, and preach again the "old-time religion," would be to turn off the present generation and to miss the opportunity which the universalist mood offers the followers of Jesus in today's world. In the universal world culture which is emerging, Bible Belt Christianity is not likely either to produce the most qualified missioners—however strongly motivated—or to gain an extensive hearing. It is not incidental that the greatest opposition to full constitutional rights for the Negro, for example, is encountered in the Bible Belt of the United States. Or that opposition to open housing in northern suburbs is frequently led by fundamentalist preachers whose churches maintain an impressive budget for overseas mission.

For the fundamentalist rarely faces the fact that his presentation of the Gospel alienates substantial numbers of men from Christ just as it wins others. There is no way to measure this. We do not keep statistics of those who refuse the Gospel. We do not number those who find the Gospel irrelevant because our presentation had made it appear so. It is too easy to suppose when the Gospel is refused that it is because of its intrinsic offense, of which the Scripture speaks, when in reality, the offense that turns the hearer aside may lie in the messenger or the vehicle of the message.

I am always irked when I turn to a particular well-known gospel radio station for up-to-the-minute news, always professionally presented in crisp current jargon, and at the close am treated to a verse of Scripture in King James English. It is not the verse of Scripture I object to. I welcome it, for I love the Word myself. It is rather the peculiarly incongruous insistence that it be given in 1611 English—and *that* on a news program reporting events that happened only minutes ago! The predictable effect on hearers who didn't grow up on the King James version must be to turn off the dial—the very effect the news bait was designed *not* to achieve. Richard Shaull writes tellingly to this point:

> It is possible to contend, of course, that contemporary human experience is profoundly anti-Christian, and that modern man simply cannot accept the Gospel. But we must

make every effort to be sure that the scandal he confronts
is that of the Gospel and not the relic of a past form of
acculturation of Christianity. Otherwise we may in effect
turn away from the church those very people who are
most responsive to what Christ is doing in the life of man
and the world today.[6]

Evangelicals of every stripe have emphasized that Jesus is
Savior. They have been less emphatic in insisting that He is Lord.
Yet the New Testament almost invariably puts it "Jesus Christ,
Lord and Savior," making it quite clear what is the biblical sense
of priority of emphasis. That some evangelicals are facing the
challenge of universalist thought to traditional evangelical doctrine is evident in statements like the following:

A gospel that is limited to a chosen few, that is hedged
about with consciousness of election and exclusion, must
be widened to include the broader promises and prophecies
of God in the ultimate accomplishment of His redemptive purpose.[7]

This can be accomplished, as Shaull seems to suggest—and
permit, I think, the simultaneous recovery of a strong sense of
call—by recapturing the eschatological perspective of the New
Testament. This should not be too difficult for an era faced with
the triple prospect of nuclear annihilation, suffocation from pol-
lution of its atmosphere and water supply, and world-wide star-
vation from a logarithmic population explosion that threatens its
food supply! The eschatological perspective insists that "God's
action in the world has something of the quality of 'mystery'; it
constantly pushes beyond the limits of our human understanding
of it."[8] This quality of mystery extends to the life of the church,
which God frequently disrupts as he pushes it "toward a fuller
and freer participation in his wider purpose."[9] The church is
God's representative community in the world, "the provisional

representation of the whole world of humanity," as Karl Barth puts it, as justified and sanctified in Jesus Christ. As such it is oriented toward the future, a future that is already becoming a reality in the present.

The eschatological perspective further saves us from an undue orientation toward success, for it recognizes that He who gathers a chosen people also disperses them in a rhythm known only to Himself. This is seen repeatedly in the history of Israel, and it is always related to the judging and the saving of the nations of the world. There is much current breast-beating about the fact that the non-Christian population of the world is increasing faster than the Christian population, and that we therefore seem to be falling behind in evangelization of the world. This is a hard fact, and not to be taken lightly. But it need not be a cause for despair. The church is called upon to follow her Lord to crucifixion, which precedes resurrection. Her current dying, from the biblical perspective, is but the prelude to a great harvest. "A grain of wheat remains a solitary grain unless it falls into the ground and dies; but if it dies, it bears a rich harvest" (John 12:24 NEB).

But die she must. The religious ghettoism that marks much of modern church life is under God's judgment. In the words of Isaiah: "It is too light a thing that you should be my servant to raise up the tribes of Jacob and to restore the preserved of Israel; I will give you as a light to the nations, that my salvation may reach to the end of the earth" (Isa. 49:6 RSV).

I am convinced that the current strong note of universalism in the church today is the Holy Spirit's antidote to the kind of exclusivism which has made Western Christendom content and comfortable, and that therefore, paradoxical as it may seem, it can be an ally rather than an enemy to the recovery of Sentness. We will see how more clearly when we examine the significance of secularization in the next chapter.

Part III

The Way Back

Chapter 7

ACCEPT THE WORLD

We have heard a part of the world saying "Missionary, Go Home!" We have heard another part as surely saying "Missionary, Come Back!" Each is a qualified invitation, with few exceptions, addressed to a certain kind of person: "Go home unless . . . Come back if . . ." To the former there has been a substantial response. Many former missionaries *are* staying home. How do we respond to the latter? Is there a way back? And if there is, what is the way?

The first requirement, it seems to me, is to accept the world. There is a sense in which the kind of Christian most likely to respond to the missionary call is often the kind who is least at home in the world. He is more likely to derive, as statistical evidence increasingly shows, from a fundamentalist sect than from an historic church. He is likely to see heaven and earth sharply polarized, and to interpret the New Testament injunction to "love not the world" (I John 2:15 KJV) in terms of that polarity. If today's missioner has become uncertain of his role and suffers from a loss of image, it is in part due to a failure to understand that he is a leaven that leaveneth the whole lump. He has tended to see himself as helping the Holy Spirit to create multiple small breakfast rolls, well raised, nicely circumscribed, browned and buttered, little bodies of Christ, His scattered church on earth. He has not really believed that his presence was actually leavening the whole lump.

Secularization, that intriguing and rapidly accelerating phenomenon which is the mark of our time, is forcing him to realize that this has happened and is happening whether he likes it or not. And the process is irreversible. There is no returning to the old kind of sacral community that marked man's societal structure until secularization destroyed it. Technology, the handmaiden of secularization, will see to that.

The missionary may react with despair or joy, depending on his temperament. He may see in secularization the summation of apocalyptic biblical eschatology and await with fear or elation the pressing of the nuclear button—the moment for God the patient Redeemer to act as God the implacable Judge. Or he may ask himself, "Is God Author and Shaper of this too? And if He is, where do I come in?"

I think the answer to the first half of his question is "yes" and that the first answer to the second half of the question is "Accept the world!"

The apostles had to learn this lesson, as Philip Zabriskie reminded the National Student Christian Federation at an assembly in Athens, Ohio, in 1964.[1] The Holy Spirit used a dream to teach it to Peter, their leader. It is recorded for us in the tenth chapter of Acts, in an account told in great detail by the Gospel recorder, Saint Luke. The emphasis he puts on the story is an indication of the radical importance of Peter's revolutionary discovery. For that dream was a turning point in the life of the church, as significant as Pentecost—changing it from a small Jewish reform sect to a church with a mission to all the peoples of the earth. Zabriskie makes the interesting point that Luke, who wrote two books that were in effect Part I and Part II of his account, begins his story in Jerusalem, the Holy City, in the Temple itself, and ends it in Rome, the secular city, the center not of Israel, the people of God, but of the whole inhabited world. And Luke ends his account there with Paul alive and preaching, free and unhindered.[2]

In Acts 10 Luke tells us that Peter was visiting with a friend, Simon the tanner, in Joppa. One Cornelius, a Roman centurion, a good man who was a seeker and a worshiper of God, was told by an angel to send his servants to Joppa to invite Peter to Caesarea, so that he might hear what Peter had to tell him. Peter in the meantime had gone up to the flat roof of Simon's house for a nap. He was hungry as well as sleepy and soon dozed. The Holy Spirit chose in that physiologically advantageous moment to visit him in a dream, and Peter dreamed about food. It was a natural enough dream—like dreaming about steaks and apple pie in a fox hole—but a strange one. A great sheet, gathered at the corners to make a bag—in the manner used by countless shoppers in public markets throughout the world—was let down before him, containing all kinds of animals. A voice said, "Rise, Peter; kill and eat" (Acts 10:13 RSV). But Peter, being a good Jew (as were all the Christians up to then) and strict in his observance of Jewish dietary laws, refused the invitation. These animals were alive, with their blood still in them, creeping and unclean, and he would not offend God by accepting the offer, even though he was hungry. "I have never eaten anything that is common or unclean" (Acts 10:14 RSV), he insisted. Thereupon the voice declared, "What God has cleansed, you must not call common" (Acts 10:15 RSV). As though for emphasis, it happened three times.

Then Peter woke up, wondering what his dream meant. He was not to puzzle long. The messengers from Cornelius arrived just then and he went with them to Caesarea. Like Jonah before him, and like countless messengers of God after him, he was almost discourteous when he met Cornelius. "I shouldn't be here, you know. After all, a Jew doesn't eat with a Gentile" (Acts

10:28, paraphrased). And as the world so often does for the ungracious Christian witness, Cornelius quietly ignored the affront and welcomed Peter. So Peter told him about Jesus and Cornelius believed and the Holy Spirit fell on them all.

Now Peter had a problem! After huddling with his Jewish companions he decided to baptize Cornelius, because he didn't know anything else he could do. Then he crawled back to the Jerusalem establishment and sheepishly explained what he had done and why he had done it, telling the whole story. Peter's experience, Luke tells us, changed the whole history of the Christian church, freeing it from its restraining ties to Judaism, and making it a church with a universal message to the whole world. Peter was soon to renege, but already (Acts 9, the conversion of Saul), the Holy Spirit, who knows the beginning from the end, was preparing his chosen Paul for the larger task of world evangelization.

Rise, Peter, kill and eat! "If this is a determinative story about the Christian world mission—and I think it is" (declares Zabriskie)—"the first missionary command is not to go anywhere or say anything, but to take the world and receive it."[3] It is an invitation to accept one's own humanity and that of one's neighbors, remembering that Jesus defined the stranger as our neighbor. It has a festive note, like that of the father of the Prodigal son, who for joy shouted, "Bring the fatted calf and kill it, and let us make merry!" (Luke 15:23 RSV). It invites the Christian to accept the life God has given him and to participate in the life of the world of which he is a part. The whole story is a glorious affirmation of life and the world, peculiarly relevant to the current issue of modern secularization.

When Peter went to Caesarea, reluctantly, he discovered that the Holy Spirit was already at work there. He had gone before, and He was entirely recognizable by His acts as the same Spirit who had blessed Peter and his compatriots at Jerusalem. It astounded him, even as it astounds us, to discover that the Holy

Spirit is already at work in the world to which we bring the story of Jesus. But that is what the Word says, and that is what we know deep within ourselves, in those moments when He frees us from our own ethnic pride, and we realize in humility that He who sends us out always goes before us.

The first step then in Christian mission is to accept the world—freely and wholeheartedly, and to rejoice in every evidence we find of God's prior activity, whether in the church or the world. And for the twentieth-century Christian this means to accept both the fact and the process of secularization. This does not mean that we ignore the danger of secularism, which is a new and false religion. It means rather that we adopt an attitude toward the world which we might call "Christian secularity." Perhaps we should define terms. Thomas E. Clarke makes the necessary distinctions clear:

> 1. By *secularization* I mean the process by which, over a period of many centuries, and indeed throughout the history of Christianity, with increasing acceleration in recent times, values and institutions of a political, economic, cultural, and, in brief, this-wordly nature have been disengaged from the direct and hegemonic control of institutional religion and Christianity.
>
> 2. By *secularity* I mean the attitude of mind and style of life which look upon the process of secularization with favor and sympathy, for whatever reasons.
>
> 3. By *Christian secularity* I mean the attitude of mind and style of life of the Christian who finds in secularization not only no threat to the Gospel, but a legitimate and even necessary explicitation of the Gospel regarding the relationship of the Church and the world, the Kingdom of God and the city of man.
>
> 4. By *secularism* I mean the attitude of mind and style of life which consider God, Christ, religion as irrelevant for man's this-worldly concerns.[4]

I should like to illustrate what acceptance of the world means by a somewhat detailed incursion into an area of missionary activity in which I have had personal experience—medical missions. For one of the clearest expressions of secularization is the development of secular medical services throughout the world —a phenomenon which would not have been possible on the ontocratic base of the ancient religions of Asia and the animist societies, but which owes its development to the widespread penetration of the world by the Christian Gospel.

Missionary medicine has tended (and in many places in the world continues) to occupy a position strikingly similar to that which obtains in the New Testament situation, where it is declared that in the coming of Christ a new power, the Kingdom of God, has entered the world, dethroning all evil earthly powers, including those to which disease is attributable. Healing is a manifestation of this dethroning, and authenticates the message. Thus the work of the Christian missionary doctor manifests and validates the preaching of the Gospel.

All healing is of God. "I am the Lord, your healer" (Exod. 15:26 RSV). Healing is *Christian* when it is done in the name of Jesus Christ (e.g., Acts 3:6). It is to be done in love, and is accompanied by the preaching of the Gospel (Matt. 10:7–8). With the widespread establishment of secular medical services, however, the dethroning of the "powers" that cause disease takes place *apart* from faith in Christ, and Christian medical missions tend to lose their uniqueness.

There are those who mourn this development, and not a few suffer intense frustration from it. Others welcome it. Dr. Shoki Hwang of Taiwan, for example, declares that it is not the business of the church to compete with what is in fact a fulfillment of her own work. We should not try to run a better hospital than the government. We should rather rejoice that because medical missions pointed the way, the government of Taiwan, for example, now runs fifty hospitals where fifty years ago there were none.[5]

Christian medical missions and secularization have together made widespread the benefits of modern scientific medicine. And the record of their achievements is a magnificent one. We scarcely need to detail that record here. The population explosion about which we now fret is ample evidence of our success!

Impressive as the achievements of scientific medicine are, however, they leave something to be desired. For one thing scientific medicine shares with technology a tendency to reduce all processes to mechanics. And the mechanization of healing, which meets some protests in our own technologically oriented culture, is something people with a non-scientific world view can ill accept. It is not surprising, therefore, that the African patient, while he may at first embrace the benefits of the Western doctor's pills, injections, and surgery, may end up rejecting modern scientific medicine. He may turn on the one hand to traditional medicine, or, on the other hand, to the faith healing offered by the indigenous Christian sects, both of which better meet his total need in the context of his world view, which regards the cause of disease as essentially spiritual. Such rejection indicates, writes Robert Mitchell, "the African protest against the materialism and secular context of much Western medicine, and a search for methods that recognize the wholeness of man, and restore the relationship between healing and religion."[6] The African, in common with most non-literate peoples, believes that it is possible, by supernatural agency, to inflict evil upon mankind. "Consequently, in every form of disease which refracts and distorts the reason, in all that is strange, portentous, and deadly, he feels and cowers before the supernatural."[7]

The Western missionary, Mitchell points out, generally failed to recognize the objective reality of the powers of evil which, in African society, manifest themselves in such things as witchcraft. Instead he concentrated his attention on moral evils such as polygamy, which, in the traditional African social structure, were not considered to be evil at all. He further taught his conception of evil to the African clergy with the result that too often these men were unable to deal directly with what were the real existential issues facing their people, such as the threat of illness and death through magic and physical means. Government medicine in turn meant secular medicine, which leaves out the deliberate invoking of the help of God. Both these failures contributed to the growth of the independent, indigenous church movement, which restores the traditional relationship between medicine and religion.

> Working in the framework of traditional causation, a framework which is still very relevant to most . . . [Africans] who believe in the power of witches, they offer comfort and safety through an authoritarian charismatic leader, a dramatic ritual and the opportunity to escape from threatening environments. In so far as they link sickness to personal sin they offer their patients the opportunity to achieve a measure of personal balance through the catharsis of confession.[8]

A belief in the *reality* of witchcraft makes many illnesses thought to be supernatural in origin unamenable to Western medical techniques. Any physician who has worked at all extensively in Africa has seen patients die without physical cause, simply because they *believed* in the irreversible effectiveness of the curse placed upon them. The witch-doctor therefore continues to have a role to play, for "in illnesses with a psychosomatic origin, such as an anxiety state . . . contact between patient and *nganga* is much closer than between the patient and the Western doctor."[9] In addition it must be admitted that many of the native practitioners' herbal remedies are of value and in accord with scientific method. Rauwolfia was used in Africa, for example, long before Western medicine discovered it as a tranquilizer. Furthermore, even if modern scientific medicine were completely adequate to the treatment of African illness, its facilities are limited. Many an African reporting sick waits all day, even days, unless he is an emergency case. It can hardly be otherwise in an area of the world where the ratio of physicians to the population ranges from one in 10,000 to one in 200,000.

What does it mean to "accept the world" in such a setting? The answer is not simple, for in attempting to meet the simultaneous challenge of secularization and the resurgence of pre-scientific medicine, be it that of the indigenous Christian faith-healer or the witch-doctor, the missionary physician faces the temptation either to reduce scientific medicine to a gimmick for the saving of souls, or to reduce his personal religious faith to simple humanitarianism.

Thus some Christian missionary physicians feel that the scientific medicine they have been privileged to learn is merely a means to an end, a gift of God to be used to attract people to hear the preaching of the Gospel, in the hopes of inducing the conversion of their patients. Missionary physicians holding to this view may insist on beginning every day at the hospital or dispensary with a religious service. The audience is essentially a captive one, and the practice invites the prostitution of the practice of medicine.

The revolt people feel against being thus used is a recurring theme in the poetry of both Haitian and African poets of the colonial and post-colonial eras, who see the church as clearly linked with the Western colonial governments in forced tutelage. The chanting of the pater noster, for example, is in their view an attempt to obscure the cry that wells from the throats of those who work the plantations under forced labor, their foreheads wet with the holy water of baptism.[10]

Nonetheless, the responsibility to present the Gospel verbally as part of the ministry of healing is not to be glibly dismissed. The spoken word has power in Africa, and failure to speak the word of Power may be failure to heal. As we have already seen, this very failure in part accounts for the burgeoning of the independent African churches, with their frequent emphasis on faith-healing.

Other missionary physicians regard their work solely as a service given to men, in the name of Christ to be sure, but without the direct intent to proselytize. The question of conversion they leave to the missionary evangelist or hospital chaplain. They feel that their function as a Christian witness is to practice the highest level of scientific medicine possible. An extreme expression of this view is given by Davis:

> Evangelization is cure of sick bodies, of broken-down, inefficient, and eroded farms, of illiteracy, of insufficient and unbalanced diet, unsanitary homes, impure drinking water, or a subsistence level of existence, of filthy villages, of the moral, mental and spiritual stagnation of corrupt practices and conditions.[11]

This view is also not without dangers. The physician motivated solely by humanitarian considerations frequently lacks the spiritual resources to relate effectively on a sustained basis to what is often a frustrating situation. And neither he nor his evangelistically oriented missionary colleague can dismiss their responsibility for the effects of a modern medical ministry. As Dr. van Leeuwen notes incisively:

> The "cure of sick" bodies makes a backward village community absolutely dependent on the resources of modern medical science, which are among the greatest achievements of our secularized world; it brings down the death rate and upsets the traditional stability of social life; it

creates fresh needs and fresh wants; it lays the village open
to a money economy and the world market—the sole agencies through which a "cured body" can go on providing
itself with the means of enjoying in the future the same
standard—or, if possible, even a better standard—of physical security.[12]

Most of us who practice missionary medicine accept the
tension of this polarity of *kerygma* and *diakonia*, rather than
choosing up sides, feeling with Wilkinson: "Christian doctors
and nurses stand before the sick in a dual capacity. They are the
trained representatives of scientific medicine, but they are also
members of the Church of Jesus Christ, and as such are charged
with a commission to heal the sick in His name."[13] In accepting
the challenge of living in this tension we must be prepared to accept the responsibilities for the effects of both evangelization and
humanitarianism, including the inevitable secularization of the societies with which we choose to identify.

It is in such self-examination that the answer to both the
challenge of secularization and the temptation to escape the tension of his dual role as a missionary and scientist lies for the missionary physician, for it suggests the cultivation of that humility
which is common to true faith and true science. Clearly one of
the lessons the Holy Spirit had for Peter in his Joppa dream
was the lesson of just such humility. And for the twentieth-century disciple, a ready acceptance of the discipline of human ecology, learning to know and appreciate the patient's world wherever he may live, agreeing to treat the patient as a person, offers
common ground to medicine and religion.

Human ecology is the study of the total man in his total environment. To scientific medicine it brings the insistence that
sickness and healing function in at least four inter-locking
spheres: physical, mental, social, and spiritual; and that in any

given illness the etiology may be multifactorial—somatic, psychic, constitutional, genetic, social, cultural, religious. Unquestionably man's beliefs about himself and his environment determine to a large extent his interpretation of health and disease, govern his response to life crises, and determine the method of therapy to be used in resolving them. To the missionary doctor working in Central Africa therefore, human ecology brings the awareness that the patient presenting himself at the clinic may simultaneously be hyponourished, parasitized, detribalized, and sinful, in need of protein, instruction in hygiene, acceptance into a new community life, and a Savior, and not simply a worm cure or herniorrhaphy or tranquilizer.

The problem of infertility is illustrative of the importance of an ecologic view. Barrenness is a serious problem in Africa. I opened a sterility clinic at the Wasolo hospital in the northern Congo in 1954, for example, which met each Monday. By the end of three weeks I closed the register and cried "Halt!"—over 500 women had registered. One treats infertility primarily as a gynecologic problem, by necessity. But the barren African woman faces a problem which brings into question the very meaning of her existence. Declares Mitchell: "Barrenness is a complex and frustrating complaint which produces a high degree of anxiety. Women are prone to try any promising remedy for it, particularly one which offers protection against the jealous witches who are blocking her womb."[14] Perhaps that is why a simple D & C (dilatation of the cervix and curettage of the uterus) was the most popular procedure in our clinic—it provided visible evidence of unblocking.

In the African world view, health is related to the life force, the central principle, the world energy of which man is a part, to whose influence he is subject, and which he may on the other hand influence himself. Fagg, summarizing the findings of Father Tempels among the Baluba of the Congo, writes:

African thought is conditioned by their ontology, that is, their theory of the nature of being; for them being is a process and not a mere state, and the nature of things is thought of in terms of force or energy rather than matter; the forces of the spirit, human, animal, vegetable, and mineral worlds are all constantly influencing each other, and by a proper knowledge and use of them a man may influence his own life and that of others.[15]

There is a basic unity in such a world, and it is precious to the African. Thus Nida can say: "No distinction can be made between sacred and secular, between natural and supernatural, for Nature, Man and the Universe are inseparably involved in one another in a total community."[16] In such a world view health is quite simply having the fullest vital potency, and sickness by contrast is any diminution of vital force. It may be caused by another's curse, by visitation from the shade of a neglected relative, or by one's sins. Explains Mitchell:

In modern Western thought sickness is generally thought to be caused by either physical or psychological causes. In traditional African thought, as in pre-scientific Western thought, these are joined by a third all-persuasive aspect of causation, the supernatural. This is the realm of spirits and divinities, of evil and witchcraft, of God Himself. This is not to say that African traditional medicine is totally supernatural, in its methods and diagnosis. . . . But in traditional healing the genuinely therapeutic and magical are almost inextricably intertwined and certain illnesses are thought to be entirely the product of supernatural agencies. . . .[17]

The practitioner to whom one submits is accordingly a priestly mediator between the living and the dead, who may simultaneously offer herbal medicine and a supernatural interpretation of the illness, with guidance for cure. He is at once a reasonably skilled botanist and a keen judge of human behavior. He is sought out because the patient feels he himself lacks power to deal with his illness and seeks to add power by establishing contact with powers outside and around him which he can influence in his favor through a skilled intermediary. That intermediary can be and often is the missionary physician. It is easy enough to fill the role when all that is required is a D & C, or Caesarean section, or a shot of penicillin. But what if it means being a Priest of God? Does the medical missionary dare to accept his African world in such a circumstance? I was once asked to undertake the treatment of an African patient whom I diagnosed (in 1954) as a catatonic schizophrenic. I was unable to accomplish anything on her behalf through the methods available to me as a Western physician. On ward rounds one morning I was told simply and earnestly by an African nurse-aide that in the village from which she came it was commonly believed that she had an evil spirit. His comment forcibly reminded me that I was an ambassador of Christ, and that Jesus had empowered his disciples to cast out demons in His name. I decided to give it a try! That afternoon I read several of the accounts of exorcism recorded in the New Testament. The one about the demon resisting the disciple of little faith (Luke 9:40) sent me trembling to my task just before nightfall. I returned to my patient and in the presence of her family and the nurse-aide, spoke to her in the manner of a first-century disciple of Christ exorcising an evil spirit. She was restored at once to her normal self, and the following morning she and her family worshiped with us in our mud and thatch chapel. I doubt I should try this as a therapeutic measure in Chicago, for Chicagoans function in the context of a world view quite unsusceptible to such a technique. But for that particular patient in Africa it was the thing to do. For the good of my patient, I accepted her pre-scientific world (so like that of the Old and the New Testament incidentally) and God honored my concern for her.

The healer-patient relationship is a person-to-person relationship, the *sine qua non* of missionary medicine, and to be impersonal is to be in a measure non-healing. The patient must never be a mere object, either a case to be cured or a soul to be saved. "By treating him as a person I help him to become one. This . . . seems to me to have particular importance today when man finds himself so gravely depersonalized by the mechanization of life and the 'massification' of society."[18] So writes Dr. Paul Tournier, who has helped so many people to wholeness. The busy physician is tempted to forget this however, be he missionary to Congo, or Chicago practitioner. The result in Chicago may be that my patient has his next consultation at the psychiatrist's office. In Congo he turns to the Christian faith-healer, or to the witch-doctor, who "in psychotherapy . . . is far superior to the scientific doctor who unfortunately tends to show little interest in the patient's family and background and so loses the confidence he could easily gain by a more friendly contact with his patients."[19]

From the posture of his embrace of both the scientific medicine in which he is trained and the pre-scientific medicine to which his immersion in a primal culture and his Christian faith alike require him to be sympathetic, the missionary physician knows that pre-scientific medicine and scientific medicine are not incompatible. They are two sides of the coin of healing, particularly when that coin is stamped "In God We Trust." Illness and anxiety are God's reminders to man of his historic situation, which is one of dialectic tension, which we call good and evil, and which scientific medicine may identify, for example, as antibodies and viruses in specific instances, but which in other instances it fails to identify. It is this failure that reminds man that he cannot escape from his responsibility to be a human being, but must confront the dichotomy in himself and in his existence.

Pre-scientific medicine, while it has its share of charlatans, often shows a higher regard for human personality than scientific medicine, which, for example, increasingly manipulates human personality through tranquilizers. We have not always performed our responsible task when we have tranquilized our patients. We may in fact have harmed them by keeping them from a confrontation that may have been more truly healing. This is always a danger in modern therapy, where the great fallacy often is that we give drugs or perform operations to relieve symptoms that are calling for existential help to meet ultimate situations. It may, in fact, be more important to teach a man to live with his illness than give him rest and ease.[20]

The healer lives in the same situation and shares the same dynamics as his patient, and they act together to achieve health. The healer therefore has the responsibility to relate as a *person* to his patient and convey to him the strength to meet his condition. Good therapy is not the same as alleviating the symptoms. Real therapy assists the patient to assume responsibility to combat the evil forces arrayed against him, be they germ or allergen, demon or shade, resentment or guilt. Declares the Tübingen Consultation with boldness:

A concept of health which is merely that of a restored balance, a static "wholeness," has no answer to the problem of human guilt or death, nor to the anxiety and the threat of meaninglessness which are the projection upon human life of the shadow of death. Health, in the Christian understanding, is a continuous and victorious encounter with the powers that deny the existence and goodness of God. It is a participation in an invasion of the realm of evil, in which final victory lies beyond death, but the power of that victory is known now in the gift of the life-giving Spirit. It is a kind of life which has overcome death and the anxiety which is the shadow of death. Whether in the desperate squalor of over-populated and underdeveloped areas, or in the spiritual wasteland of affluent societies it is a sign of God's victory and a summons to His service.[21]

Prayer does not therefore stand over against penicillin as a therapeutic means. Prayer helps the patient acquire confidence that the forces arrayed on his side are stronger than the forces arrayed against him. Furthermore, it helps the physician by increasing his own confidence, helping him achieve the insight into the problem before him for which his scientific training has prepared him. Granted, one cannot pray with every patient. But one must be sensitive to the Holy Spirit's leading. For not to pray may be to convey to a patient one's rejection not only of one's own professed faith and of his world, but of him as a person.

Finally pre-scientific medicine also reminds us of the role of the supportive community in the healing process. My patients in Africa were brought to me surrounded by members of their family, carried in emergencies in a fish net suspended from a bamboo pole borne on the shoulders of loved ones. Their wives and sisters and mothers came along to cook for them during their stay. It made for some problems in hospital logistics, but I would be hard-pressed to make a case for the superiority of the ambulance and the central kitchen in that particular African setting. The loving concern of others is a great incentive to recovery from illness. Africans understand this better than we who have worshiped so long at the shrine of Western individualism. That we suspect the truth of it is evidenced by the loosening up of hospital visiting hours in our own country over what obtained a few years ago.

Where the community is one in which the members have found healing and strength in God, knowing themselves to have been spiritually ill, and now forgiven and made whole, restored to fellowship with Him and each other, the therapeutic force is tremendous. Such a community the church can be, offering prayer, worship, the Sacraments, indeed, the laying on of hands and anointing, even exorcism where indicated. And to those who are aliens to the world in which they live, their alienation identified in addiction to alcohol, narcotics, LSD, or other drugs; or paralysis, blindness, mental illness, or old age; or diseases requiring prolonged therapy, such as leprosy, the church owes the full measure of her capacity to care. In accepting this charge let her do so in humility, accepting all the wondrous aids which modern scientific medicine makes possible. And let scientific medicine, on her part, accept the church as her partner, recognizing as legitimate the church's claim that man must be treated in the totality of his sickness, including the dimension of spirit.

It is possible to accept the world and remain Christian. Indeed, one cannot be an effective Christian today without doing so. And what is true for the practice of medicine is equally true in the area of education, or agriculture, or radio evangelism, or community development, or literature distribution. When we accept our world and participate in it as the place of God's activity and man's redemption, we discover that secularization is our ally, and technology our friend, even as we discover that, wherever we go, God the Creator and Christ the Redeemer have gone before.[22]

Chapter 8

PITCH A TENT

The first step on the way back to mission is to accept the world which God has created, rejoicing in every sign of His activity in it and in His church, including the fact and process of secularization, with all that this implies for the Christian mission. As we do so one of the first discoveries which we make is that one of the consequences of secularization is the re-emergence of the New Testament diaspora, a fact of enormous significance for the evangelization of the world and the penetration of the Gospel into secular life. It is God who gathers and God who scatters, so declares the biblical account from Adam through Abraham and Nehemiah to Paul. Today there is a vast scattering of the people of God, made possible through great technological break-throughs in transport, and with it there has come a concurrent revolution in communication. Some 2,000,000 Americans alone go abroad annually. Less than one in forty go out as missionaries in the formal sense. But at least half name the name of Christ in a measure, and a sizeable number must actually be committed Christians.

What has the scattering of the people of God to say to mission? Is it simply an accident of our times, coincidental to the technological revolution, unrelated to the purposes of God? Or is it truly a part of his grand design, a miracle of multiplication of missionary loaves for the feeding of the soon-to-be five billion?

The professional missionary is indeed *persona non grata* in some quarters. But there are few areas in the world where the skilled technician is not welcome, and fewer still where he is not admitted. And where the Dutchman may be hard to take for reasons of history the American is likely to be acceptable, or vice versa. So with the Frenchman and the Englishman. With the exception of the countries behind the bamboo curtain, there is hardly a spot to which a Christian offering a sought skill may not go, there to share both his skill and his faith.

Yes, both his skill *and* his faith! Most of the rest of the world doesn't have the American and European's hang-ups about personal witness. Where we are frequently embarrassed to talk about our personal faith, except perhaps to join in discussions about religion in the vaguest of terms, much of the rest of the world finds it quite natural to discuss religion in quite specific and personal terms. Free from the Western dichotomy of the sacred and secular, now suffering a hard death from the onslaught of secularization even among us, the Eastern believer in Hinduism, for example, readily shares his faith.

One of our hang-ups is, of course, a false understanding of tolerance. The longing for peace and harmony is an understandable and commendable longing, of course, especially in a world where the population explosion combines with the proximating effects of technology to bring mankind into a rapidly developing state of enforced togetherness. And it is a longing with deep religious roots and sanctions. Tolerance makes for unity, even where, for want of will, mutual understanding is lacking. Religion falls into deserved disrepute where tolerance is lacking. Furthermore, the desacralization of society which secularization is effect-

ing has in a curiously paradoxical way increased the demand for
tolerance, for humanitarianism seems to have a more universal
appeal (for modern man at least) than religious injunctions,
which seem more subject to the insidious effect of bigotry than
non-sacral humanitarianism.

Arnold Toynbee, who admits himself to be rather more
Eastern than Western in his religious position, is a prime protag-
onist for tolerance in the dialogue between religions, and he has
had great influence, since he writes well, and is widely read, and
because, no doubt, he projects so well the mood of his times.[1] But
to be tolerant is not enough. And when tolerance demands as the
price of dialogue a prior surrender of all claims to uniqueness on
the part of all parties engaged, the price is too high. This is so,
not merely because it denies the exclusiveness inherent in the
Christian's claims for the Incarnation of Jesus Christ, but also
because it arbitrarily repudiates a fundamental factor in human
culture, which even UNESCO, which bends over backwards to
be humanist without being in any way religious, has had to recognize; namely, the factor of religion, from which culture has been
inseparable in the history of man, at least to the present.

Thus Hendrik Kraemer, to whom I owe the main lines of
the above argument, can write of the "fatuousness of 'neutral-
ity,'" which, while capable of pursuing a mutual appreciation of
cultural values in a multi-cultured world, is unable to provide
the motivation for "radical, unforeseeable reorientation and
self-revision, which leads to facing anew the question of truth."[2]
And nothing less can save the world. No, it is not enough to be
tolerant.

The seriousness of true religion demands that one shall be
really *one's religious self* (italics mine) and avoid the temptation . . . of putting as an indispensable condition of dialogue and relationship the assumption that all religions are

essentially one. As an axiomatic assumption it robs all true religion of its seriousness. This seriousness need not hinder participants from being open to new insights through the instrumentality of contact with one another.[3]

To be "really one's religious self"—and there can be no true dialogue where the self is denied—requires for the Christian the continued assertion of that exclusiveness which is intrinsic to the Christian faith, in spite of the implied offense. New Testament Christianity readily admits to the offense: "but we preach Christ crucified, unto the Jews a stumbling block and unto the Greeks foolishness" (I Cor. 1:23 KJV). To be inclusive is not necessarily to be more humble, as Kraemer sees so sharply in a footnote on "the terms of the Coming Dialogue":

> An intriguing point in relation to the offense of "exclusiveness" is always that the Hindus especially, in the name of "inclusiveness," are thorough exclusivists in a concealed way. That is, by their claim in regard to "inter-faith relations and conversations" that "inter-faith relations" should mean that the "Christian arrogance" of offering by the Gospel the normative concept of religion should be dropped at the outset, and the tenet of the one, universal religion, hidden in all religions, should be taken as the normative concept. They have, of course, a perfect right to maintain this latter position, but it is really strange that they do not see how such a demand at the outset that one of the partners in the inter-faith relation should surrender his true position is arbitrary dogmatism and a frustration of genuine interfaith relation: a flight from the real issue.[4]

A part of the problem of tolerance is the Western Christian's reaction to a sustained period of defense against charges of imperialism and notions of superiority on his part. We are trying so hard not to appear imperialistic or guilty of any feelings of superiority, that we hesitate to share any firm convictions, lest we be accused of domination or bigotry. A concern to be humble and avoid any semblance of arrogance, including religious arrogance, is laudatory. But there is a confusion here, a kind of packaging in one ball of wax of mixed components of one's culture and his self. A conquering by witness is not of one piece with a conquering by force. Conversion of a people by presentation of the claims of the Gospel is not of itself an act of imperialism. While we may apologize for our part as Christian participants and inheritors of our civilization and nation's history, we need feel no guilt that former animists became Christians in the process. *That* we must see as part of the mystery of God's acting in history, and we can rejoice in it in the same breath that we apologize for the slave epoch.

The mood of apology with its crippling effect on the capacity of Christians to bear witness to their faith is abetted by a growing aggressiveness on the part of emissaries of the other world religions which, in its turn, also has cultural components. Newly independent nations are proud, and rightly so, of their new-found selfhood. Their religions share in this sense of pride, and in pressing their claims on the descendants of their former Christian masters, produce in these heirs a kind of uneasiness. There is always the temptation to bow the knee to Baal, whenever and whatever Baalim manifest secular ascendancy.

The essence of the problem really lies in a kind of uncertainty about what we truly believe, and a doubt about its relevance either for modern man or for people of other cultures. The Christian claim for exclusiveness, eroded, as we have seen, by a false understanding of tolerance and an almost masochistic apology for past sins "has nothing to do with religious arrogance, intolerance or dogmatic absolutism . . . it rather includes a real openness to truth wherever it may be found, and an inclusiveness of its own sort, far more realistic and adequate to the human situation than the superficial, glittering universalist theories of the East and of theosophical and philosophical syncretists."[5]

Christian laymen, as distinct from the professional experts occupying chairs in comparative religion—who for their part are surely obligated to develop a new *apologia* for the Christian faith in a secularized, multi-cultural world—may well be the key to the recovery, not only of Sent-ness, for which we have already pled, but for a new understanding of the essence of our faith, expressed in terms pertinent to our times. It is they who are fully and daily involved in the vast enterprise of theoretical and applied science in every field of human endeavor. It is they who "are not only intellectually but existentially confronted by the demand to spell out their faith in correlation with the new adventurous realm of apprehension of world, life and man, implied in the elusive term 'modern world.' "[6] And an increasing number of this vast host of Christian lay people are part of the new diaspora, fanning out, establishing bridgeheads, infiltrating (if you will) the farthest reaches, geographical, cultural, social, political, economic, and scientific, of our globe.

And there is reason to hope for a recovery of certainty about the things we hold to be true. For there are very real signs of renewal in the church, including her laity. Dr. Eugene Nida describes some of these in his book *Religion Across Cultures*, in a chapter significantly entitled "From Man to Man." The story he tells about Don Venancio, a Mexican Indian whose life and witness as a Christian layman is a classic example of redemption at work in a man and a community, gives the lie to the "God is dead" theme. In Don Venancio we see God at work in the "redemption of people's hands,"[7] beginning with the simple witness of one traveler to another, and ultimately including the transformation not merely of this one man, but of his whole commun-

ity, spiritually, socially, economically, and spilling over to community after community in contact with the first in the Valley of
Tasquillo.

The Laymen's Leadership Institute in our country is an example of a formally organized program that teaches people in
business and the professions how to experience and share the
reality of Christ in home, business, society, and church. Hundreds of such cell groups of believers meet with inquirers from
every vocational group and level of life and gather regularly
from such formal structures as well throughout our land and the
world. These cell groups cross denominational lines and include
both clergy and laity in a growing movement, whose numbers
cannot be counted. The magazine *Faith At Work*, which Nida
describes as "so modern as to be suspect by the staunchly ortho-
dox, . . . so evangelical as to make it questionable to the liberal
left,"[8] reflects the tenor of the movement perhaps as accurately
as any single publication can.

In Indonesia, the immediate aftereffect of the attempted
Communist coup in 1965 and the subsequent fall of Sukarno
has been a huge turning of the disillusioned of that land to Christ.
Signs of renewed activity by the spirit of God are widespread,
and it is significant that it is occurring at the very moment of a
great scattering of His people, largely unplanned by pope or
bishop or mission board, but occurring with a spontaneity and
simultaneity indicative of the hand of the Holy Spirit. Surely
He is scattering us, even as He also gathers! And herein lies the
great hope of mission in our time.

The lay missionary movement, as it is usually called, is a
phenomenon to be watched, nourished, and encouraged. It goes
by several names, each of them objectionable in a measure. "Lay
missions" is the common term, but it confuses the issue, since
many laymen, as opposed to clergymen, serve as regular or professional missionaries. "Non-professional missions" is also used,

but it is likewise confusing, since many lay missionaries are people qualified in the professions. I like the term "self-supporting missions," since it defines the lay missionary at the point of true distinction: He is a person motivated by mission, but unrelated to the traditional sending bodies. He is a free agent, who supports himself. His sources of support may be expatriate, of course, as in the case of a foundation representative, for example. Or they may be local, as in the case of a technical adviser to a national radio system who is paid by the government of the country where he works and lives. But the self-supporting missionary is unrelated to the power structure of an ecclesiastical body. He is therefore less subject to the cry "Missionary, Go Home!"

Eric Fife and Arthur Glasser, in *Missions in Crisis*, devote a chapter to "Rethinking the Non-Professional's Role," discussing the advantages as well as the disadvantages of the self-supporting missionary. One of the points they make is that "in some countries that are hostile to the gospel, refusing to admit conventional missionaries, Christian teachers and engineers are welcome. In other countries from which Christian missions have been expelled, 'nonprofessional' missionaries have been permitted to remain."[9]

Every country in the Third World shares a desire for technological advance, and all are concerned with education. The scientist and teacher are respected members of the community, and the personal witness of such a person is heeded. An awareness of the potential for mission represented by this new diaspora has grown rapidly among both Christian leaders and the man in the pew in recent years. Dr. Paul Rees, in an editorial in the February 1968 issue of *World Vision Magazine* entitled "Christian Infiltrators" reflects on the challenge presented by growing opportunities abroad in the most unlikely places for just such missionaries. Basing his editorial on a particular instance of opportunity in Nasser's Egypt, which was advertising in foreign journals for technical and professional assistants in certain of its government departments, he raises a probing question:

> Here then—in Africa, Asia, and Latin America—are places where the unconventional missionary has an opening. Not a big opening, nor a frequent one, but an opening just the same.
>
> Have we Christian infiltrators who are prepared to move in?
>
> When it comes to the forms of Christian witness, new ground must be broken, new entries made, new chances taken.
>
> Too long have Christians in African and Asian countries given the impression that they are an island of piety, scarcely washed by the seas of the nation's surrounding life and action. Foreignness can never be completely disclaimed by the expatriate from Europe and North America, but something can be done to lift this stigma from the Christian community in mission. Perhaps infiltration in the spheres of business and government is one way of doing it.[10]

Infiltration may not be the best word. It may smack too much of the CIA and Cold War intrigue to capture a generation of followers of the Galilean carpenter grown weary of Viet-Nam and conflict in the Middle East. But it is not unbiblical. "Be wise as serpents and innocent as doves" (Matt. 10:16 RSV), our Lord counsels His disciples. To be at once wise and innocent is the missionary's dilemma in any era; it is particularly so in this post-colonial, post-Constantinian one. And yet it is a dilemma more truly congenial to the self-supporting missionary than his professional colleague, who often finds himself not a little ill-at-ease in being associated with the sending body of a powerful American church.

A few years ago a consultation of theological schools in

Southeast Asia called on its members to prepare their students for a possible life of self-support apart from the pastoral ministry, declaring that "such a so-called tent-making ministry should be fully recognized and honored by the church, as a ministry to which men are called and in which they need to be upheld by the prayers of the Church as a whole."[11] The French Reformed Church in 1967 asked its Board of Theological Education to make proposals on the possibility of theological students training for a trade or profession before becoming pastors.

Certainly a "working" clergy would save the financial situation for many a struggling church too mired in the sheer weight of supporting a full-time staff ministering to its own local needs to dare to launch into mission beyond its immediate borders. It would fill the developing gap between churches and preaching posts needing filling and the supply of a trained clergy to fill them. It would further contribute to the death of the myth that mission is but one facet of the church's life, best relegated to an élite corps of ecclesiastical professionals.

This image of the clergy is of recent date, as Steven G. Mackie reminds us, and without clear biblical justification. "Indeed the profession as we know it was not a sociological category in New Testament times."[12] We have made much more of the fact that the early Jerusalem church accepted the apostles' complaints about not being called to wait tables, but to preach the Word (Acts 6:1–7), than we have of the equally biblical reference to Paul's being self-supporting. Acts 18:3 tells us that Paul was a tent-maker, and earned his living as such. He himself tells us that, although an apostle had a perfect right to accept a stipend from the community, as Peter did, he himself "availed myself of no such right. On the contrary, I put up with all that comes my way rather than offer any hindrance to the gospel of Christ" (I Cor. 9:12 NEB). When he came to Corinth he accepted a partnership to that end with two persons of the same trade, Aquila and Priscilla (Acts 18:2).

Having one's needs fully supplied by a distant supporting and sending body can in fact be a hindrance to the Gospel. The stipend may be all out of proportion to local standards (the average missionary evangelist is vastly better paid than his co-workers in the indigenous church) leading to envy and inhibiting real communication and identification. On the other hand, where a church is growing rapidly, as in a genuine people's movement, the insistence on a paid clergy may stifle the movement or otherwise shoulder the young church with an impossible financial burden. In such instances basic biblical training for the lay leaders of the multiplying congregations and ordination to a voluntary and unpaid ministry is a solution that both preserves the impetus of numerical growth and provides adequate spiritual nourishment to assure the emergence of a true church. In Africa teachers in primary schools often serve such a role. French worker-priests are a contemporary European counterpart, as are worker-clergy in American cities who take a job with city hall. At a more sophisticated level, one may cite the lay-preacher status of Astronaut Frank Borman in the Episcopal Church. The rapidly developing theological extension programs of evangelicals in Latin America, in which Ralph Winter of Fuller Theological Seminary is a moving force, are another case in point.[13] All these examples are efforts to bridge the hindrance to cultural penetration which often afflicts the professional clergy. The gap is even more apparent in the case of bright young men taken from African churches and sent to European or American seminaries for training, returning after many years to the leadership of churches from which they may have become widely separated in outlook during their absence.

To advocate a tent-making ministry is not to reflect negatively on the value or work of full-time professional clergymen or missionaries. It is simply to admit, on the one hand, that being paid to be religious can be a hindrance to the Gospel; and on the other, to seize opportunities for mission that must otherwise go begging. For the opportunities are there. Writes R. Park Johnson:

> The American churchman who lives and works abroad faces an exciting opportunity for Christian service. The layman or laywoman overseas, even on a temporary assignment, may be just as effective a Christian missionary in the real sense of the word as the regular professional worker on career service in the church's mission enterprise.[14]

He may even be more effective. The fact is that the demonstration of a Christian life whose character and purpose and dedication reflect a deep sense of mission in the midst of a non-Christian environment, apart from the having to do so that is expected of a professional missionary, may accomplish a most effective witness for the Gospel. Mr. Johnson quotes a non-Christian friend, who was impressed by the influence of a Christian friend, as saying: "Oh, we expect the missionary to act like a Christian. After all, that's his job. But this man doesn't have to!"[15]

To those who would object: "True, the self-supporting missionary may *live* as a Christian but he's not as free to *witness* as the professional missionary," we should have to admit that for certain categories this may well be true. Certainly, if he represents the American government, the United Nations, or the Peace Corps, for example, he is not free to be an active proselyter, particularly in a country like Egypt or Israel, say. But he is not under compulsion to hide his faith. I fear that far too many Christians who go overseas are only too glad to find an excuse to rationalize their inability to witness to a faith poorly understood and tenuously held. As we have suggested above, the people in the country where they work are probably free from hang-ups about saying what they believe, and may even interpret such silence with scorn, not crediting non-witnessing Christians with tolerance as they hope, but rather dismissing them as crass opportunists seeking favor by soft-pedaling their own faith.

This is not to say that one can or should be belligerent about his faith, or dissipate his work-time in deliberate efforts to create opportunities to witness. Humility and respect for others and a sensitive waiting upon the Holy Spirit are essential elements in any witness to personal faith. But given the opportunity, one will rarely offend by expressing quietly and with sincere conviction what he believes. He will rather be respected and give credence and meaning to the life he has already shared without words. There are examples in every country of American Christians like that. If there were more such, "the whole mission of Christ's church in the world could take on new vitality and convincing power."[16] Perhaps the cry "Missionary, Go Home!" was necessary to make us realize that "we have so magnified the call from Macedonia heard by a few that we have failed somehow to hear the same call spoken to every man who accepts Christ."[17]

One upon whom this dawned with real force in 1957 was R. B. Kochtitsky, founder of LAOS, "Laymen's Overseas Service." His was not the first of such organizations, and today there exist at least two score, representing structured attempts on the part of various denominations, groups, and individuals to channel the growing response of those who are hearing. LAOS is an uncommonly good choice of a name for such an effort—for the *laos* is the people, the whole people of God, whose new life in Christ ought to thrust them into the world, there to serve the *laos*, the people of the earth, and witness to them of the Creator's grace in Christ. My own denomination (the Evangelical Covenant Church) calls its self-supporting mission effort COV—"Covenant Overseas Vocations." Whatever the name, the *raison d'être* is similar—to steer the laymen of the church into mission in today's world. Declares Kochtitsky:

"The changing world must be met by the servant people living one day at a time in radical openness and in the revolutionary faith which knows the difference between form and content."[18] LAOS and similar agencies attempt to put the content of the Gospel into new forms as formless as possible, recognizing the flux that marks modern life, while striving to retain the uniqueness of missionaries, which lies "not in a special kind of elevated status" but "in the integrity of their humanity and their commitment in love and joy to a life of service."[19]

I do not write from a position of non-involvement, for I have personally worked as an employee of the Democratic Republic of the Congo. The opportunity came in August 1960, shortly after the Congo became independent from Belgium. The Belgians left the country in droves following mutiny in the army and among them were most of the physicians who staffed the impressive hospitals scattered throughout the land. My wife and children were evacuated too, under orders from our Board of World Missions, and I was left as the sole physician in the Banzyville territory, a region as large as the whole of Belgium and with a population of 100,000. There were three hospitals in the territory—the 100-bed Catholic hospital at Wapinda, our 50-bed hospital at Wasolo, where I was stationed, and the state hospital at Banzyville, with 200 beds. There were in addition five leprosaria in the territory, ten dispensaries, three tuberculosis sanitoria, and some thirty injection centers for leprosy. I was invited by telegram from the provincial capital of the Equator Province at Mbandaka (Coquilhatville) to assume the responsibility for the medical services of the territory, residing at Banzyville. It was an opportunity to become involved in a new way in the life of an emerging nation, needing help in a period of near chaos, and I accepted.

I had numerous interesting experiences as *médecin territorial*
of Banzyville, which I cannot detail here: like setting the tumblers
in the lock of a new safe which had arrived at the administrative
offices of the territory after the departure of the Belgians and
the instructions for which were printed in German. *That*, like
most of my experiences during the several months I was there,
was a thoroughly secular one, though not amoral. For after setting the tumblers, I taught the administrator himself to set them,
and then asked him to reset them by himself when I left, so that
if any funds disappeared no one could blame the new *monganga*
(doctor)!

I remember many things about the experience, quite apart
from the enormity of the task, the ceaseless stream of the sick,
and the endless travel from one end of the territory to another.
There was the joy of acceptance and a new freedom to share my
life and witness from a different power base, not extraneous, but
indigenous to the people I served. At last I could not be accused
(as I had once been) of being paid to witness to the grace of God
in Christ. The government of the newly independent republic
was not about to employ a man whose task was Christian testimony! I was touching people with whom my contacts before
had been rare, including in addition to the neglected poor the
neglected influential, people in government and professions
whose acquaintance I had largely been denied. I moved about in
the *world* as distinct from the church, and the church itself included not only the Protestants in whose circle I had worked for
many years, but, in a new way, the Catholics, who now saw me
in a different light. Nor did my Protestant connections suffer
from the move. The struggling evangelical community in Banzyville was proud to count the chief medical officer in the territory
as a part of its congregation, and held its chin a bit higher for the
increased respectability they had suddenly gained. This is not un-
important in some areas—I think chiefly of Latin America where

evangelical Christians have long suffered from an inferiority complex. Moving more freely in the "world" and in "higher circles," I was more exposed to the crosscurrents of developing Congolese society, and became more sensitive than I had been to the political, cultural, and economic trends of the country in which I bore my witness and did my "thing." I continued to spend part of my time at the Wasolo hospital, and to participate in the life of the church and in the councils and activities of my missionary comrades. But I was released from many of the tedious and trying details and annoyances associated with a missionary's life in a jungle mission post, with a consequent improvement in my own sense of well-being, which, I am sure, made me a better companion, and as a consequence, a more consistent witness to God's grace.

The precipitous arrival of independence to the Congo brought a host of such opportunities. No mission board, including mine, saw the import of them, or if they saw them, moved to fill the vacuum. I wrote an article for the *Covenant Weekly* pleading for a seizure of the hour. It fell on deaf ears. Not only in the area of medicine did the chance occur. The opportunity in teaching was even greater. As Fife and Glasser report with sadness:

> At the very time when a vast body of missionaries were being withdrawn from the Congo, UNESCO appealed for 300 salaried teachers to man the Congo schools. Only 131 volunteered, and there was not an American among them. Without ignoring the formidable difficulties facing a teacher in Congo, one would conclude that a core of well trained and spiritually effective teachers could have exercised a powerful influence for Christ, even though conventional missionaries had been withdrawn from that troubled land.[20]

The day of opportunity is not past, for although increasing numbers of doctors and teachers are being produced in the Third World, the technological gap between the rich and the poor nations is widening rather than narrowing because of the logarithmic character of change. It is to be hoped that Christians, showing in the midst of atrophy growing signs of renewal, will rise to the challenge. For the Christian layman today, Mordecai's words to Esther are prophetic: "Who knows whether you have not come to the kingdom for such a time as this?" (Esther 4:14 RSV).

Chapter 9

ALL THINGS TO ALL MEN

It is Paul, the first overseas Christian missionary, who suggests to us where the road back lies. Of the numerous passages where he does so the most fascinating is that very personal ninth chapter of I Corinthians. "Am I not an apostle?" he begins. "Am I not free?" (I Cor. 9:1 KJV).

That question—at least the first half of it—was raised for me in the second person when I returned to the Congo after a prolonged absence and found myself once again relating to the church in which and for which I had personally labored for a decade. It had suffered from the post-independence struggle for ecclesiastical power and from the *Simba* rebellion. It had also known the grace of growth. And it had problems. One of them was finances. At the risk of repetition let me return to an incident mentioned briefly in Chapter Four.

The Wasolo region had always led the other regions of the Church of Christ in the Ubangi in proportionate giving. But the region had suffered from neglect on the part of the central church leadership. There had been a series of church treasurers, who, if not guilty of actual embezzlement, were at least guilty of weakness, with all which that implies in a culture where the extended family makes anyone who holds a bag of money an easy victim for a "touch." The church leaders came to me for counsel. I was reluctant to interject myself into the situation, fearful of encouraging a paternalistic role that would ultimately weaken rather than strengthen the church. I expressed my reluctance to the African leadership. After a pause the question came: "*Ojali ntoma te?*"

"Are you not an apostle?"

I was brought up short. The question and the tone were in a measure accusative, and I was forced to reconsider my role as a missionary. To be missionary—is this not to be apostolic? "Whatever you bind on earth shall be bound in heaven" (Matt. 18:18 RSV). Were these and many other words of our Lord addressed only to the Twelve, or at the most the Seventy? Or was the unconscious recognition on the part of the Congolese church leadership that my foreignness and the part I had played in bringing them the Gospel gave me a right—indeed a duty—intrinsic to the role of missionary a true biblical insight?

When Paul raised the question, he followed it immediately with a second: "Am I not free?" Was *I* not free—free to speak, free to act, free to share whatever gift the Holy Spirit had elected to give me, even in this situation so charged with a short but full history, so symbolic of the confrontation of the new and the old, so pregnant with the cross-fertilization of two epochs in transition, so rich with my own personal struggle for meaningful identity as a human being and a servant of Jesus Christ?

My hesitation was natural and perhaps a good thing. It was natural because I had lived in that very spot through a period of colonial history, independence, and post-independence in the Congo, and was conditioned by that experience, plus extensive travel, reading, and exposure to the councils of mission executives, to be sensitive about doing anything that might smack of missionary imperialism. It was a good thing because there could

be no turning back of the clock. Yet by the same token I could
not afford to freeze in a position that seemed to suggest that I
was shutting myself off from the church. They could only interpret such a stance as a kind of inverse paternalism, a post-
colonial position taken by too many Western Christians, easy to
rationalize, but as un-biblical as the former variety.

I was not being asked to make a decision *for* the church.
Nor was I being asked to carry out a decision *under* the church.
The church had in a short and tumultuous history moved from
*de*pendence to *in*dependence. Each period had known its own
kind of excesses and neither was wholly faithful to the biblical
understanding of the body of Christ. The church was asking me to
join *with* them in coming to a decision. It was now asking for
*inter*dependence. It was asking that they, the Congolese patriots,
and I, the expatriate, be one in the body of Christ, sharing our
gifts in a mutual effort to win their nation for Christ. How hurt
they had been when, as a committee met for the fusing of the
mission and church charters (which meant, in effect, the death
of the mission organization), one missionary, after refusing an
offer of full membership in the Ubangi, also refused to become
an associate member! The strained silence that greeted his re-
fusal was broken by the sigh of a Congolese lay churchman
who said: "I used to refuse to believe it when my friends who
went to the States came back saying your churches in America
don't accept black people as members, because I knew *you*. Now
I believe it!"

The missionary had justified his position on the grounds that
he belonged to the church at home and was just a counselor in
the Congo. The Congolese were saying in effect: "We're tired
of *counselors*. You're always holding yourselves back, keeping a
safe distance. We want *you*, and we want you to be a full par-
ticipant in the life of our church. You've been Christians longer
than we, and have more experience in things of the faith. You've

lived with the Word of God longer. We want you to share your gifts with us."

To be apostolic means several things. It means that the missionary is more than what he is. He is what he is *plus* his Sentness. To deny this is to betray one's calling with a false humility. It is to go to a place without going there, and to live there without being there. To be apostolic is to be foreign. The missionary is always a foreigner, whether he goes from suburban America to the ghetto of an American city, or from rural Kansas wheatlands to the Congo. Jesus was a foreigner from heaven, rejected by the only people who could claim him as a national for not being a nationalist. Seeking a home wherever people would welcome and receive him, he died at their hands on a cross, at once victim and victor.

The missionary, as Dr. Robert Lee so aptly describes those who in that role go to Japan, is and remains a "stranger in the land."[1] In Japan his strangeness derives from the transcendent character of his Christian faith, as against the ontocratic character of ancient Japanese traditions where nature and the divine, the state and religion are identified as the woof and warp of the same piece of cloth.

But his very foreignness may require the missionary to speak. The Congolese were saying, in effect: "You, who were not our people, came to us with the message of God, the Good News of the Gospel. You did not come to us because your own land is not beautiful. Our friends have seen the marvels of your country. You came because God sent you. And because He sent you, you must speak when we do wrong." In this they were speaking out of a biblical context. "If your brother sins," commanded Jesus, "rebuke him" (Luke 17:3 RSV).

To be apostolic means to carry a kind of authority intrinsic to one's call and self-awareness of it. To assert it is to run great risks. But there is little real danger anymore that one of those risks is to reduce the church overseas to a satellite of the sending body. And to be silent may be to emasculate one's self, to betray one's call, and to fail to serve the church with which one has cast his lot. There is no fear to speak or write in Paul. And even in this era of exaggerated national sensitivities, we cannot abdicate apostolicity. Thus an outstanding Asian Christian declares:

> When a missionary church is reduced to the bare function of recruiting agent of personnel and finance to support another church, then the heart of the missionary connection has been betrayed.[2]

To be apostolic is to be a symbol of the universality of Christ's presence in the world. In a time of heightened nationalism, and a resurgence of Roland Allen's emphasis on tribal churches, the missionary apostle is needed more than ever as a symbol of the fact that God is neither black nor white, yellow nor brown, that He is neither Congolese nor American, nor Ngbaka nor Ngbandi, that He speaks English with as much fluency as Lingala or Taiwanese. The church is international and supernatural. It cannot live to itself, and to this apostolicity bears witness.

To be apostolic is to be catalytic, as Paul was, when he initiated a response on the part of the Gentile church to the plight of the Christians in Jerusalem. In the situation at Wasolo with which I began this chapter, I was able to be such a catalyst. I did not call a special conference of the church as I was asked to do. But I invited the vice-president of the church, a personal friend, to come from its central headquarters to the Wasolo region for a visit. He is an excellent evangelist, and after consultation with the regional church leaders, I asked him to come to the area for three weeks of evangelistic services. When he came we talked the situation over, and *he* called a special meeting—not as my stooge, I hasten to add, manipulated into doing what *I* wanted done (any acquaintance of Phillip Babese would quickly affirm *that*), but as a sensitive leader of the church who used his authority to accomplish a task he and I and the local church leaders together saw as needing doing.

In the conference that ensued, I was a *source of alternatives*,[3] bringing to the local situation the experiences of other Christians in other lands, offering thereby a range of solutions from which the local Congolese regional church could select, and which it could adapt to its own situation. St. Paul, from his wide travels and broad contacts with the churches, unhesitatingly played such a role. To be apostolic, as he was, is sometimes to be such a source of alternatives.

It is also to be a mediator, quietly and unobtrusively, with intercession and love and caring, with tact and earnestness and boldness, bringing parties in tension together. One's very foreignness is here an asset. Unrelated by blood to any of the extended families involved in the conflict, related only by the blood of Jesus mutually acknowledged, one stands as a link to forge the broken chain.

It is to be a conscience. And to be a conscience requires an exemplary life, free from impurity or disharmony in one's family relationships, or carelessness or corruption in finances, wherever one touches them, or covetousness about things or power, or coldness in communication. It does not mean perfection, but it means striving after it, a readiness to confess sin, and a willingness to expose one's self as weak and in constant need of grace. Thus one may in a measure become what is also apostolic, as Paul almost immodestly claims it—an example. Faulty, yes. Imperfect, yes. But, nonetheless, worthy of being followed, and a source of inspiration.

And to be an example is to become a challenge to others

to become their best. The church needs such challenges: people who practice evangelism, when the lust for ecclesiastical power and position takes gifted men away from the paths of witness; people who embrace a lower standard of living far from home, an encouragement to young doctors and teachers and others to identify with needy people in the bush, resisting the lure of city practice or superior employment for the sake of a better salary. (I'm not suggesting here that we don't urge young graduates to enter government service—here, however, we are concerned with motivation that leads to dedication and unselfish service.)

Yes, to be all things to all men means to be apostolic. It also means to be free.

Here I should like to turn to a discussion of method. For being all things to all men surely means a willingness to be experimental. Dr. David Stowe of the Division of Overseas Ministries of the National Council of Churches has suggested that every mission board should put twenty per cent of its total budget into experiments in mission. That seems like a very high level of risk—yet he speaks from his broad knowledge of the obsolescence of many of our forms of mission and the need to develop new methods.

Experiments *are* being made. The many current efforts to relate the lay diaspora of which we have already written to the missionary task are among the most significant of these attempts. Here the financial risk, at least, is minimal, and the resources are almost limitless. What is needed is a breakthrough in communication, a kind of dramatic self-discovery on the part of the church of its role in the world, a new Pentecost which issues in meaningful dispersion.

There is a need to be innovative in a way that captures the very real note of desire for mission which undergirds much of the rebellion among the youth of the church, for example. We react with loathing to the long-haired, unkempt hippie. But among today's flower children are to be found those who are highly motivated, who combine a search for personal integrity with a zeal to aid their fellows and to do the will of God. I thought as I passed through Haight-Ashbury when it was the true mecca of the hippie movement and observed the beggar-like youths who sat in doorways or on curbs, how like parts of many an Oriental city Haight-Ashbury was! I thought of the mendicant monks of Eastern cults, and the Christian church's own begging friars of medieval times. And I wondered: Is it impossible to believe that God could use some of these strange people in just such circumstances abroad, wandering about on the face of the earth in the name of Jesus, giving a blessing for a cup of water or a slice of bread or a bowl of rice in His name, divorced of all existential security and dependent on God alone, able to say with Jesus that they, like the fox and the bird, have neither hole nor nest (Matt. 8:20), free from all identification with the Western power structure that has to date so tainted our presentation of the Gospel?

That hippies feel a kinship with the East is undeniable. Their literature, wedding ceremonies (when they have them), and interest in Indian gurus alike testify to a kind of at-homeness on their part with the East which to date has largely escaped the West. In being all things to all men, do we dare to let the hippie rediscovery of the freedom in witness which non-employment (in the formal sense) gives a man, be put to use in mission?

That is perhaps an extreme example. Paul speaks of being a Jew to the Jews (I Cor. 9:20). My own denomination, together with a Mennonite group in this country, and other Christians in Switzerland, Holland, and Germany has experimented in dialogue with the Jew in Israel through what I think was a most imaginative attempt to be a Jew to the Jews. A community called *Nes Ammim*—"an ensign to the peoples"—has been set up on 260 acres of farmland fifteen miles northeast of Haifa, modeled after the Israeli *moshav*, or cooperative community. Essentially agricultural, it expects to become self supporting. The *kibbutz* and *moshav* have been a distinctly Jewish pattern for settlement of Jewish immigrants to Israel and for development of the country's land. In an article in the *Covenant Companion*, Reverend Russell Cervin described the goal of *Nes Ammim*:

> The articles of incorporation for Nes Ammim USA emphasize the concept of "bridging" and say in part: "(We purpose to) establish a new kind of Christian presence and service, and to provide a continuing basis for interaction through the establishment of a Christian community development project in Israel, thereby erecting a sign of love and reconciliation in accordance with the Gospel of Jesus Christ."[4]

Dr. Jacob Bernath, Swiss, and a leading spirit in the project's founding, writes of the community as "a token of indebtedness to Israel. It is with shame and distress that we admit the innumerable persecutions of the Jews in past centuries." He sees *Nes Ammim* as a "token of brotherhood. . . . As Christians we are united to Israel through our Lord Jesus Christ, who was born of this nation, died and rose to life again in Israel. Also we are linked to Israel by the Old Testament, and we pray to the same Father. . . . Our object, as we see it, is to be brothers in Christ to the Jews, desiring to live as such with them, as the servants of our Lord in obedience to his word."[5] *Nes Ammim*, at this writing, is less than a howling success largely because brotherhood among the Christians themselves in this international community of individualistic Westerners has been wanting. It has now become essentially a Dutch project, which, it seems to me, is unfortunate. But the idea remains a great one, and the attempt to be a "Jew to the Jews" worthwhile.

Paul also writes of becoming "to them that are under the law, as under the law, that I might gain them that are under the law" (I Cor. 9:20 KJV). How, indeed, does a Christian witness in a land where the law forbids his witness? How, for example, in Muslim lands of the Middle East? How does one become, in a sense, Muslim, in order to reflect Christ to Muslims? Surely the need on the part of Muslim lands for Western technical assistance in education and industry, indeed, in government itself, is an *entrée* that we have scarcely attempted to use.

Or, further, "to them that are without law, as without law" (I Cor. 9:21 KJV). This passage took on genuine meaning for me for the first time during those hectic days in the Congo immediately following independence, when overnight every man became a law to himself; when, in the words of Judges, "every man did that which was right in his own eyes" (Judges 17:6 KJV). And often the right was terribly wrong! I was glad then, living without my wife and children at Wasolo and Banzyville, commuting on roads where one was frequently stopped by official and unofficial roadblocks and subjected to intensive and senseless questionings, some harassments, and occasional indignities, that I was indeed alone. For anarchy ruled, if rule it is. And I envied my Roman Catholic priest friends their celibacy! They had only their own skins to be responsible for.

This is not the first call for a Protestant celibate corps. Others have suggested it, and formal calls for single men have gone out. The Methodists, for example, called for fifteen young celibate men to join their Congo staff during the period of turmoil which gripped that land and turned the assets of family life into liabilities. And it comes, curiously, when the leading subject of bull sessions in Catholic seminaries is whether or not to marry!

But a highly mobile, multilingually trained corps of young unmarried men, well disciplined, and possessing broad skills in administration, communication, and personal relationships, together with specific technological skills, could serve a very real need in this age of frequent revolutions and political upheaval. They would have to be expendable, as paratroops and commandos are, but the risks are really not great, and surely less than those facing soldiers in Viet-Nam. They could well include widowed missionaries whose children are grown, or husbands from grown families where the wife shares in mission by her willingness to be separated for a time. These would have the advantage of "auld acquaintance" and knowledge of local languages and culture. And there is a large pool of such people, some of them very much alive and retrainable for specific tasks. Not a few would just as soon leave their bones abroad as at home. In certain instances they should be women, self-possessed people with no hang-ups about their bodies, aware of the risks involved, but willing to accept them, and to contribute their presence and skills in delicate situations where they could do a better job than men.

We Protestants may not be up to it. Even Catholics are having growing doubts about celibacy themselves. But the kind of élite corps we are describing would of necessity be ecumenical, and Catholics have far more experience in celibate living than we. Surely this is an area for dialogue and experimentation. And in an era when increasing numbers of Protestants and Catholics are joining common cells of Bible study, prayer, and service, an experiment in a common corps of Christian commandos, ready at a moment's notice to fill a critical need in an area of turmoil, deserves a try. When Paul queried, "Am I not free?," he posed a question for which an affirmative answer is sometimes easier to make on the part of an unmarried apostle. Celibacy poses its own problems. But it does not require a man to make a decision that may result in the violation of his fifteen-year-old daughter, with the resulting deep scars which such trauma may inflict, both on her and himself, as well as others whom they both love. Violence is not likely to diminish in the immediate future, and violence against our race bids fair to increase. In the face of such facts a church serious about its mission to the world must admit that to be free may in some instances require celibacy; and admitting it, to implement the obvious.

When Shadrach, Meshach, and Abednego were cast into the fiery furnace, they discovered another one present in their midst, whose face was like the Son of God. They were in the fire, and He was there with them. And they came out alive! It may not be exegetically sound, but I would point out that in the place of fire, it was Shadrach, Meshach, and Abednego—*three young men*—who were there. The church today, facing conflagration here and there, needs its trios of young men. And I dare say they too will find the Presence in the midst of the furnace.

Such a corps should be international, as United Nations peace-keeping forces are. Much has been said about internationalizing missionary forces, and a start has been made. The Oriental Missionary Society, for example, is developing international teams for purposes of evangelism. World Vision–sponsored pastoral conferences often feature an international staff. Obviously a commando-like mission corps sent to hot spots of the world would of necessity be international, were it to have any chance of acceptance.

It struck me in visiting Indonesia, where large numbers of former Muslims have become Christian that Indonesian missionaries should be functioning in North and Central Africa, particularly as professors serving with others from Europe and America and Africa on the faculties of theological schools. What a help they could be to the rest of us, whose knowledge of the Muslim faith is so limited, and particularly to animist Africans who face making the choice between Christ and Mohammed.

Some years ago, Herbert Jackson of the Missionary Research Library made a plea for the planting of Christian monasteries in lands where such social service structures are common expressions of the indigenous faiths. It was a call for renewal of an ancient Christian pattern very familiar to the Middle Ages. His call led to no great response. Perhaps the project in Israel— *Nes Ammim*—was a kind of response to that plea. The Christianizing of the Hebrew *kibbutz* idea is a kind of modified monasticism.

Another such response is the Jesus Abbey, described by Roy E. Shearer in the November 1968 issue of *World Vision Magazine*.[6] Here, in a remote, nearly inaccessible mountain valley in Korea, Koreans, foreigners, Christians, non-Christians, military personnel, diplomats, and missionaries of all denominations come to seek spiritual refreshment in an atmosphere of warmth and love. Founded by Father Archer Torrey, an Episcopalian minister, the little community of thirty-eight offers spiritual renewal to people of all walks of life through prayer, worship, and hard work on an eighty-acre farm located in the Tebek Mountains of Kongwon Province. Here young men, women, and couples come to live and learn what following Christ means in the everyday give-and-take between individuals. Training is also given in pioneer rural evangelism, so that the participants return to their life in the world able to share their new-found or newly refreshed faith. Jesus Abbey is making an impact on the people of Korea, both national and foreign. It could well be a key to a modern method of mission, an adaptation for our age of ancient monasticism. Among Catholics, John A. Bell, W. R., reports that the Capuchins in the Congo

> are now asking themselves whether or not they should seek to introduce into central Africa the style of life led by St. Francis and the early Franciscans. Traveling bands of preachers living in villages among the people rather than

in monasteries, ministering to the sick, to those in prison, living on alms from the local people or by manual work. Not engaging in strictly parochial work, but revaluating the original Franciscan charisma in the present day conditions of central Africa which, from a sociological and religious point of view, resemble more the Europe of the Middle Ages in which the Franciscan ideal was born than our present Western world.[7]

One of the most important rediscoveries of our era is that made by Roland Allen of St. Paul's missionary methods. Allen's interpretation of Paul, made sixty years ago, has become the cornerstone of the School of Mission and Church Growth at Fuller Theological Seminary, brought there by Dr. Donald Mc-Gavran from Eugene, Oregon. A stream of studies on church growth has poured from the pen of Dr. McGavran and men of similar views, such as Bishop Pickett, as well as their students. A genuine concern for scholarship and a strong association with the disciplines of theology and anthropology has lifted the church-growth thesis above the hobby level to a serious and respectable school of thought which is having great impact on mission planning and program at all levels.

A hundred million animists in Africa alone will decide in our lifetime whether to become Christian, Muslim, or agnostic. Smaller numbers in Burma, Indonesia, Oceania, India, and Amazonia will make similar decisions although from a different set of choices. With the Bible now translated in its entirety into 210 languages and the New Testament into 270 more; with modern means of transportation bringing all the tribes within reach of a personal presentation of the Gospel; with transistor radios and literacy coupled with available literature making penetration of even isolated homes possible; with the disease peril that decimated nineteenth-century missionary staffs virtually eliminated; and with churches planted everywhere, it would seem that rapid church growth is a very real possibility in these areas. Churches like the Pentecostalists of Chile, Brazil, and Mexico demonstrate that rapid church growth can and does happen. The Disciples of Christ have seen impressive growth in Puerto Rico and the Congo, as have the Presbyterians in Taiwan, for example. Church growth *can* happen. But it is not likely to happen unless we see it as a topmost priority and are willing to put large resources of personnel into responsive areas. There *is* a dust principle in mission, and there is a Macedonian call. Had Paul not recognized both it is doubtful indeed that the West today would occupy the place it does, not only in Christian history, but in technology as well.

One could wish that the emphasis on church growth had come to the fore forty years ago, for the areas where church growth principles, as described by Dr. McGavran, have their most fruitful application, that is, among animist cultures, are fast diminishing. Unless these principles can be proven to apply just as effectively to labor groups, ghetto societies, and professional bodies which constitute the homogeneous cultural units of modern pluralistic society, it may well be a case of too little and too late.

Dr. McGavran has taken a normal and avid American interest in statistics and put it to the service of evangelism. So applied it becomes a useful antidote to an excessive accent on the individual, which often characterizes both pietistic evangelicalism and liberal "social gospel." And it has helped to make acceptable to Christians the recent application of computer aids to our missionary task. MARC, the Missions Advanced Research and Communication Center in Monrovia, California, a ministry of World Vision International, is one such development. CARA, the Center for Applied Research in the Apostolate, is another. The former is evangelical, the latter Catholic.[8] Both do mission research, clarifying purposes, evaluating means, using the precise projections of statistical data to forecast likely trends in rapidly changing social structures, digesting and making useful vast amounts of information. There is a very real sense in which such efforts at using modern technological tools is being all things to all men that by all means we may save some.

There are many others—the imaginative use of radio and television in developing countries, for example. The Evangelical Covenant Church, with a grant of funds for radio work in the Ubangi, chose rather to develop a recording studio (Studio ECCO) in Kinshasa, capital of the Democratic Republic of the Congo, putting its facility at the disposal of the Congo Protestant Council, preparing programs for airing on the Congo national radio. That decision now makes the ECCO staff representative of all of Congolese Protestantism in Tele-Star, the country's new national radio and television facility in the capital, together and side-by-side with the state and the Catholic Church.

Such instances of interchurch and church and state collaboration are increasing, and represent another growing edge of new forms of mission. At Boende in the Congo, the Disciples of Christ, the Catholic Church, and the provincial government cooperate in a common medical effort. The latter furnishes the facility, equipment and supplies, and indigenous staff. The Disciples supply doctors, and the Catholics nursing sisters. This seems to me to be an instance in which genuine recognition is taken of the impact of secularization on our age, a sincere attempt to maintain missionary presence in an area of national life—the healing services—where the church can make a unique contribution.

Paul also declared that he became weak to the weak (I Cor. 9:22) and that he had become a servant to all. That is another dimension of mission, and to it we shall devote our last section.

Part IV

Come, and Lay Your Bones

Chapter 10

CAREER MISSION—A LIVE OPTION?

D. T. Niles, writing of his visit to Africa in 1958, reports a conversation with Africans about the kind of missionaries they felt they wanted: "Send us missionaries who will live with us, work with us, die with us, and lay their bones here in Africa. We do not want missionaries who come to shake hands and say goodbye."[1]

There is a great deal of missionary handshaking in this era of the jet plane, surveys, and short-term missions. In some instances the flood of Christian tourists who visit a "field" to "see missionary work first-hand" is of such volume as seriously to impair the work of the missionary host or national church leaders who give the royal tour of the various posts and installations. There is substantial value in such visits although frequently the main value is to the visitor himself. Often he returns an enthusiastic supporter of overseas mission where he had been lukewarm at best before. His eyes are opened and his vision enlarged, and he gains a new perspective of the church's task. Sometimes he returns critical, which may or may not be good, depending on what he has seen and how accurately he interprets it. Whatever the value to him personally, or to the Church in the homeland to which he reports, or to the mission itself, whose course he may as a consequence of his visit actually influence, the value to the church and staff he visits is usually limited to an expression of common interest and solidarity, symbolized by the handshake. For it is the handshake of departure, a saying goodbye, and not one of identification. It is rather like the blown kiss than the prelude to rolling up the sleeves.

So too with surveys. They are needed—we all know that— to introduce the hard look at frozen patterns, to mine the potential for better use of given resources, to shame the laissez-faire and non-cooperative spirit, to suggest the burial of dead institutions, and the creation of new forms. And sometimes they are the absolute prerequisite to the launching of a new era in mission. But survey teams come and go. They impose their probing presence on their hosts for a brief and often uncomfortable spell, leaving a wave of mixed feelings in their wake—insecurity, hope, resentment—then shake hands and say goodbye. Months, even years pass before any visible change results from the visit, and then the chief result may be withdrawal of the staff involved— inverse bone-laying, if you please.

And what of short-term missions?

They are surely one of the truly exciting developments of our time. Thousands of young people today are volunteering for short-term missionary service. And not only the young. At the other end of the spectrum a growing number of "senior citizens" sharing a common boredom with retirement and a desire to make a closing-out contribution to the life of the church are offering themselves to mission boards and asking if their skills might not be put to some use overseas. They include a wide assortment of occupations. Recently the Christian Business Men's Association, for example, established a kind of clearing house for retired accountants who offer their services at their own expense to mission boards for help in setting up books in overseas missions. Any harried mission administrator will attest how badly their services are needed! Christian physicians and dentists, serving under a variety of organizations, are making a significant contribution to overseas hospitals, relieving staff in need of furlough, filling vacancies, and supplying special skills for shorter or longer periods of service.

It was the Peace Corps more than any other force which brought the attention of the world to the value of short-term mission, as well as the enthusiasm of young and old alike for the opportunity. And doubtless the publicity given it has played a leading role in the exploding interest of the church in similar programs. But the Peace Corps did not invent the idea. The Mormon Church has long maintained the practice of sending out her young men two by two for two years. I met such a pair in Brussels, Belgium, when studying French on the way to the Congo in 1951. Certain of the Peace churches, such as the Mennonites, send their young men overseas in lieu of military service. Mennonite young men are a conspicuous segment of the American community in Kinshasa and other cities of the Third World, serving in relief operations, agriculture, teaching, construction, etc. When a program was initiated at North Park College, Chicago, supported by the students themselves, and linked with the overseas mission effort of the denomination that sponsors the school (the Evangelical Covenant Church of America) forty-two volunteers applied for five spots the first year!

But the short-term mission, for all its value in capturing the enthusiasm of committed Christians of all ages for a period of self-sharing in an overseas situation; for all its genuine contributions to the life of the church overseas, as well as the church at home, with which the returning STM'er shares his discoveries; for all its proven efficacy as a prime recruiter of career missionaries, has, nonetheless, serious limitations.

The short-term missionary usually is frustrated in the area of communication. Not knowing the language of the people among whom he works, or knowing it poorly, he finds the language barrier almost insuperable, unless he goes to a country where his native tongue is used, or unless he has a particular flair for language.

Frequently the receiving missionary or national church staff is ill prepared to use his gifts to their full, and the short-termer is frustrated by either inactivity or by substitute activities which make him feel like he is wasting his time. Or, in the case of the college student taking a year off from his studies to serve on an overseas assignment, he may have no particular skills to offer, and hangs around looking for things to do, feeling like he is in the way (which he sometimes is).

Again, the short-termer may actually be resented by career staff, who question the dedication of someone who is not committing his entire life to the mission, as they have done, and they therefore tend to regard him as on a lark. Many short-term young people are seekers, without the clear-cut convictions of career staff, and their indefiniteness about the motivation for their presence may be irksome to their more dogmatic career colleagues.

Short-term missionaries rarely get adequate orientation to their anticipated situation in advance. They seldom enjoy the same degree of prayer support and concern which a supporting church traditionally gives to career staff with which it is linked (except in those instances where a local church sends out one of its members). The limited duration of their assignment may obscure this handicap, for many can ride on their enthusiasm and spiritual capital without replenishing their resources for a time, but for some the lack of such community support may be a serious deficiency.

Neither the tourist, visiting executive, survey team, nor short-term missionary can meet the basic need filled by the career missionary. It is for this reason that the cry "Missionary,

Come Back!" continues to be heard at the same time as the contrary message "Missionary, Go Home!" and that Africans could say to D. T. Niles: "Send us missionaries who will . . . lay their bones here in Africa."

What is involved in the laying of bones in a people's soil?

This is perhaps not the place for a discussion of the mystique of soil. There *is* such a mystique, and it explains the curious tug which the soil of the Congo, for example, has on the hearts of the children of missionaries born there. It is surprising how substantial a number of missionary children return to the areas where their parents served. I am not questioning their motivation, but a part of it is surely the tug of the soil, an inner compulsion to return to where one's roots lie.

Such returning is deeply embedded in the African psyche itself. As a missionary doctor at Wasolo, among the Ngbandi people, I was frequently hard put to give an answer to the query of relatives of a seriously ill patient at the Wasolo hospital as to whether or not he would make it. If I hesitated in my reply, so that I conveyed doubt, they would likely make off with him in the middle of the night, and a man whose life might otherwise have been saved would perish. If, on the other hand, I replied too glibly, "Sure, he's going to make it!" and he subsequently died in his hospital bed, I would do them a serious disservice, for it was of utmost importance to him and them that he die in his own village.

Thus Africans who ask that we lay our bones in their soil are quite simply asking for our identification with them, or in other words, for our full acceptance of them. For to come and go, to shake hands and say goodbye, is really to say, "I want to lay my bones in my own father's soil, to die in my own village, among my own ancestors." But saying so—and it is something Africans perfectly understand—is also to admit that I never expect or want to be one of them. And this is the ultimate pathos in the symbol of bone-laying. For it suggests to the Christians at least that for all our preaching about joining a new tribe, the tribe of Jesus, we really do not mean it. We are not truly blood brothers. Jesus' blood may save us, but it does not make us one, members of a common family, whose ancestors are Abraham, Isaac, and Jacob (how often that phrase recurs in African prayers!), Paul and John and Peter.

Career mission is not merely an option. It is a continuing must. It was perhaps never more needed than in this period of growing nationalism. While we share with Dr. McGavran the conviction that the Gospel must be free to expand along natural ethnic and cultural lines so that people remain fully a people when they receive the Gospel message, we can never yield to exclusivist and racial pressures which vitiate the universality of the Gospel so central to its message of redemption. The career missionary is the necessary continuing symbol of the fact that the God who isn't white isn't black either. He who speaks Banza also speaks English. He does not lift one people simply to crush another. He would have all men saved. "For all have sinned and come short of the glory of God" (Rom. 3:23 KJV).

I do not share the sentiment of the missionary who declares, "I'm only here to work myself out of a job." He usually does not mean it, in the first place, for when a qualified national is ready to step into his shoes, he finds it hard to move over. And if he does, he will do post-graduate studies while on furlough so that he can move *up* rather than over. But quite apart from that, if he really does work his way out of a job, there remain countless other jobs for him to do, for which he is uniquely qualified. It seems false economy to assume that the moment a national is trained to do what one has been doing, one's days as a missionary are over. In most mission situations there simply is no such excess of qualified people, national or expatriate. Scores of hospitals are unstaffed by physicians in Africa today, to cite a single area as an example. They will not soon be filled with African doctors. Often the government hospital nearest them is similarly unstaffed. Yet in the current mood of anti-institutionalism we somehow manage to rationalize such situations as for the best. If hospitals have been demoted to dispensaries in order to concentrate staff in a regional teaching hospital which by its effort holds forth the promise of a better day for the people temporarily (from seven to fifteen years!) deprived of a physician's services, that is one thing. But too often lack of staff in a particular hospital that once served a large area is not related to such genuine efforts at fulfilling a larger vision at all. It rather represents a situation of default.

The career missionary is needed by the receiving church to help it meet its personnel needs. He is needed, as we have suggested, to symbolize the universal and international character of the body of Christ. And he remains a deep need of the sending church, which cannot afford to withdraw into itself. The need to do a better job at home does not abrogate the continued need to be involved overseas. Indeed, there is grave danger in the current mood to concentrate on our problems at home. Suppose every man in America does become a king, with poverty eliminated, our famous standard of living a fact of every American's life, equality of educational and job opportunities fully realized? If it is done at the expense of turning our back on the rest of the world, the gulf between us and the people of the Third World will become so great that we will become objects of far greater hate than we know today. No longer will they desire to imitate us—they will seek to destroy us. Strictly selfish motives alone require Americans to become *more* involved, not less, in the life of the world overseas. This is true at all levels. When U Thant and Uppsala alike call for increased sharing on the part of the wealthy nations with the poor nations, they reflect an awareness of our bonds as human beings that seems to escape those Christians who would withdraw our overseas forces to concentrate on the need for more consistent witness and service at home. The Western churches have not *begun* to stretch themselves. There is precious little real sacrifice, especially in the larger denominations. Those smaller churches that elicit the scorn of some and the condescending smile of others (and the grudging admiration of mission administrators in the large denominations and councils) know the joy of giving, and for all their lack of sophistication commonly have a greater concern for the spread of the Gospel among the world's peoples than their compatriots in the large churches. Western Christians are a long way from the biblical tithe, to say nothing of reaching the offering *beyond* it. We are embarrassed to speak of the low level of stewardship in the younger churches, but our own leaves much to be desired. We write a great deal about the dangers that Western money imposes on them. We write less of those dangers we impose on ourselves by keeping it for ourselves.

The selfhood of a church is not so much a function of self-support as of responsibility. Disciples of the three-self formula tend to put too much stress on self-support as the measure of indigenousness, to the neglect of self-propagation and administrative selfhood, forgetting that it is possible for one church to receive help from another both in money and personnel without losing its soul. On the contrary it is *im*possible for a wealthy church *not* to share both with another church in need without losing hers. It is not really, therefore, a question of do we or don't we for the Western churches. It is a question of how.

One obvious answer to the question is to increase the traffic in the other direction. I recognize that to do so is to subject the Western churches to the charge of complicity in the much discussed "brain drain." But it is a risk that must be taken, for only a mutual sharing of gifts can free the West from the charge of ecclesiastical imperialism, and the receiving churches from an inferiority complex. There are gifts to be shared—in art and drama and worship aids, in preaching and understanding of the Gospel— by the younger churches which, if shared with the West, would go far to eliminate the evils that are inherent in our own sharing with them of our abundant wealth. And it must go beyond to- kenism, for in a world whose dimensions are being concentrically diminished with the passing of each day, the universality of the Gospel, and the oneness of the people of God in a divided world, require clear demonstration, not only in the so-called developing nations, but in the so-called developed ones.

For the truth of the matter is that there are *no* developed nations. There are only developing ones, and we need each other. By the same token, there are no longer older churches and younger ones. All are young, or fit for burial. And only by a vastly increased mutual sharing of the gifts of the Holy Spirit can we become the body of Christ to the world. Is not this ex- actly what Paul is talking about in that graphic twelfth chapter of I Corinthians? "The eye cannot say to the hand 'I have no need of you,' nor again the head to the feet, 'I have no need of you.' On the contrary, the parts of the body which seem to be weaker are indispensable" (I Cor. 12:21–22 RSV). We have talked much about the six-continent theory of mission. We have done practically nothing to testify to its reality.

But surely one such testimony is the career missionary, who goes from one church to another, to live with its people, to work with them, to die with them, to lay his bones among them. He need not do so through traditional mission structures. Where these are suspect, or have played out their role, let him enter the life of a nation abroad and the life of the church there planted through secular structures. We have written of the lay mission- ary, whom we prefer to call the self-supporting missionary, in Chapter Eight. He too can be a career missionary, at least in some instances. I am personally acquainted with a doctor who has become the personal physician of a chief of state in a newly independent country. He has done so with a high sense of mission, and truly loves the country of his adoption and the man he serves. It would be hard to measure his influence, but it is significant. Such people are welcome abroad. They have access to circles denied the usual missionary, and are free from association with any foreign power structure. Their numbers could be considerably increased with patient effort.

Some of them should fully adopt the country where they work, that is, they should become citizens. America has absorbed many people from strange lands, and been vastly enriched for it. Of late, she has been accused of draining some of their best talent. It is time to reverse the "brain drain," to feed some able sons and daughters into the lifestream of those nations which are at the same stage of development at which we found ourselves during the great immigration wave. Perhaps this is a possible answer to the restlessness of Christian youth in the West, for whom the prospect of life in an affluent society holds little but the threat of boredom. The time is ripe. Hundreds of American young men have slipped across the border into Canada with great ease, moved by the desire to eschew or escape military service in Viet-Nam. Not a few servicemen have defected to countries granting them asylum, such as Sweden. Increasing numbers of Americans are emigrating to Australia and South Africa. The ties of Americanism, I am saying, are no longer so strong a force that the surrender of one's nationality to assume another for the sake of Christ is an unlikely option for the career missionary. It should receive far more serious consideration than it has received to date.

The decision to surrender one's nationality, particularly for Americans for whom it means the loss of identity with the most powerful nation in the world, would be a kind of ultimate step in identification, if taken seriously and irrevocably. It would in many instances require a return to the kind of existential naïveté that marked the first-century Christians. It would surely demand a genuine and wholehearted trust in God for daily securities. And such trust might well recover for its bearer something of the qualities of boldness and creative encounter which made the early Christians turn the world upside down.

But it would also confer a new freedom on those prepared to make the step. For there are serious disadvantages to carrying the passport of the most powerful nation in the world. "To the weak, I became weak" (I Cor. 9:22 RSV), declared Paul. I have sometimes felt ill-at-ease representing America. My pride in belonging in a special way to the astronauts who walked on the moon is tempered by the burden of it. And when the bombs and napalm fall on North Vietnamese villages, killing those whose way of life so closely resembles that of my African friends, I am no longer proud. I am rather tongue-tied. There is a place for silence, of course, but Good News is something to be declared, and he who would speak a word on Christ's behalf has need of his tongue.

There are precious few signs that nationalism is on the wane. It rather seems to be enjoying a resurgence. How else can one understand France, the Nigerian-Biafran conflict, Middle East tensions, and the conflict between Russia and China? Rather than bemoan the fact of it, the church, while continuing to press for the higher claims of the common humanity of the nations, would do well to recognize the validity of nationalism as a human force. And part of that recognition surely requires a willingness for some at least of her emissaries to become loyal citizens of the nations to which they bring the Gospel.

Chapter 11

MISSION AS PRESENCE

There is a poignant account in John Taylor's *The Primal Vision* with which he opens that remarkable book, about a little African schoolgirl in a gentian blue frock who becomes for him a focus for the understanding of presence as Africans uniquely know it. He describes her visit to his hut, and is moved to comment:

> It is an unfailing wonder and delight, this tranquility of human relationships in Africa. Whether it be child or adult makes no difference; one can enjoy the other's presence without fuss or pressure, in conversation or in silence as the mood dictates. Whether the task in hand may be continued or must be left depends upon a score of fine distinctions which the stranger must slowly learn; but one thing is certain—a visitor is never an interruption.[1]

It seems to me that Taylor's comment—"a visitor is never an interruption"—has profound significance to the whole intent of our discussion of the theme "Missionary, Come Back!" Whatever may be the effect of past history on the relationship of black and white, whatever modifications current nationalism may make of traditional African values, the very resurgence of those values

which an awareness of their history and the development of nationalism makes inevitable is likely to include a reaffirmation of
the African's deep insistence on the sacramental character of
human presence.

I have had occasion in personal experience to taste something of the meaning of this mystery of presence in Africa, most
profoundly grasped in moments of tragedy, including death in
the family.

We lost a child during our second term in the Congo. The
event occurred at his birth at Karawa, 400 kilometers distant from
Wasolo and the Ngbandi people among whom we worked. We
were surrounded at Karawa by the love of missionary comrades,
and felt the sustenance of their presence, expressed in all the
symbols familiar to our own culture, including a stream of brief
visits, the sharing of tears, the clasping of hands, prolonged well
beyond the brevity of normal greetings, the embracing and the
talk. There was much talking. In Western culture, particularly
the American variety, we fill the void that tragedy brings and
the embarrassment of our inability to do much about it with
talk. It runs the gamut between piety and gaiety, whisper and
guffaw, and covers a range of subjects, some, like reminiscence,
related to the event that brings the visit, but much of it trivial,
designed to avoid the event. There is hush, but there is rarely
silence. Silence is a quite intolerable thing for Westerners.

After the funeral, at which the high moment was the tear-
ful singing of the missionary children of the Ubangi Academy,
and after my wife was able to travel the rough roads again, we
made our way back to Wasolo, dreading the confrontation with
another round of sympathy. I shall not describe the scene of our
return to the people of Wasolo, who had become, as Naomi's
people to Ruth, our own in a very real way. I wish merely to call
attention to a marked difference in the way they shared our sorrow.

They would come—nurses from the hospital, teachers from

the school, village chiefs and gardeners, deacons of neighboring churches, former patients, residents of the nearby leprosy colony —often with a simple gift of a few eggs, some papaya or oranges, perhaps a chicken. But the first word spoken was uniformly the quiet announcement, made from a face masked in sorrow, sad and unsmiling, yet filled with a sense of sharing, for death was familiar to them: "I have come to sit with you."

And that is what they did. They sat. We sat together, unspeaking, and we sat long. At first the silence was scarcely endurable. My Western soul wanted to shout out: "*Say* something, for goodness sake, say *something.*" But there was no saying, or very little saying. And after a time the silent strength of their presence got through to me, and I felt the sustenance of it. I was enveloped in a community of which I was now more really a part than I had been before when I had seemed so invulnerable. White people's babies never died, you know, and a doctor's! But the doctor's son had died, and lay in Congo soil, and perhaps now he could better understand what it was like to lose half of one's children, or never to see a child born strong and beautiful come to the age of walking.

William J. Samarin, writing from a background of experience with the Gbeya people of the Central African Republic, points out that the Gbeya do not feel under obligation to talk in circumstances where we may expect it, even though they are not a taciturn people. Silence is regarded as effective as speech in many situations and more effective in some. It is, for example, the main feature of "sick calls," the function of which is to demonstrate to the family and the community that one is not happy about the person's illness. He recalls:

> I have been visited on several occasions when the first pleasure of being honored by love and concern gave way to annoyance. Wracked as I was by pain, I wanted to be

distracted by talk, but my Gbeya friends had not come to take my mind off my physical condition. They had come instead to remind me of their solidarity with me. This was achieved in silence.[2]

Ralph Harper writes meaningfully of this most difficult—for Western man—of all the facets of presence:

The atmosphere of presence, of giving, of wholeness, is silence. We know that serious things have to be done in silence, because we do not have words to measure the immeasurable. In silence men love, pray, listen, compose, paint, write, think, suffer. These experiences are all occasions of giving and receiving, or some encounter with forces that are inexhaustible and independent of us.[3]

Silence is truly a part of presence. But it is only part. Declares Taylor:

The core of Africa's wisdom is that she knows the difference between existence and presence. "Europeans," they say, "are people who do not greet one another in the street." It is easy to excuse ourselves by pointing at the congestion in Oxford Street, but that is only to endorse their critique of such a civilization. For we ourselves know what it means, as a stranger passes us on the pavement, to catch a fleeting, spontaneous smile and to know we are recognized not by name but simply for our humanity. For a moment our presence to one another, eye to eye and face to face, dispels the isolation and lifts our hearts.[4]

"Africans," he continues, "believe that presence is the debt they owe to one another."[5] "I am debtor," said Saint Paul, "both to the Greeks and the Barbarians" (Rom. 1:14 KJV). Thus

Nuntume the schoolgirl came to sit silently with Dr. Taylor as he ironed his clothes, and ended her visit with the words, "I have seen you." Thus Leon Bakuya, the nurse-aide, and Bangapa, the chief of Taragini, and Nyamazumi, the inhabitant of the Wasolo leprosy colony, came one after the other to sit with us when we lost our child. They were offering us the gift of presence. Can we Christians offer less to the world, we who stand in the name of Christ, who was Emmanuel, God present among men? Is withdrawal because times are hard, and our whiteness a stigma, and the guilt of our forefathers a burden, the truly Christian understanding of mission today? Or has presence, which Jesus enshrined in so humble a temple as a meal of bread and wine when He asked his disciples to remember Him, something to say to our comprehension of our missionary task today?

How often we have offered salvation and withheld the gift of self! If the Ngbandi remember me at all as a missionary who lived among them for ten years it will not be for any sermon that I preached, or building that I built, or road that I cut, or buffalo that I shot, or even perhaps for a desperate operation I performed to save a man's life. It will be for the night I stood by Njela Moke's grave and wiped tears from my eyes; or for the independence day celebration when I donned bark cloth and a monkey-skin hat and picked up a spear to join the marching throng that shouted, "*Vive l'indépendance!*"; or the times I seized a paddle to row with the crew that ferried my truck across the Ubangi River.

Surely one of the meanings of mission as presence is simple participation in the life of a people. Yet we are so hung up on work in Western culture that we drive ourselves to irritability in the pursuit of accomplishment and have no time for visiting with people, or for sharing their lives. We are Marthas, we missionaries, and fail to choose the better part. Isn't it time, now that so much of the *work* has been turned over to the national churches spawned by missions, that we accept this transfer as a blessing and become friends of the people we once were content merely to serve?

Friendship is a gift that makes no assumptions and no demands. It neither requires nor rejects intimacy, but it is capable of it. It knows how to listen when another speaks, and to accept a question even when one has no answer for it. It shares self without denying it, or without the necessity for apology or defense. It exudes peace in the midst of conflict, tranquility amid turmoil. It admits of difference without diffidence. It knows how and when to laugh or cry or be silent.

The day is past when mere activity, however noble, will convey to the world the sense of purpose which should mark those who declare themselves to be on a mission for God. The revolt of our own sons and daughters in the West against the WASP work ethic is surely warning enough that busyness may obscure the voice of God. And what they are saying to us in rebellion or plaintive indifference to our hopes for their futures is an echo of what Africans have long known by God-given intuition.

What Paul crystallizes for us in the inimitable thirteenth chapter of I Corinthians remains the classic summary of the meaning of friendship as presence. It is only through love that one becomes thus sensitive to others and learns the grace of receiving as well as giving. For the true friend is vulnerable, weak as well as strong, able to share his weakness as well as his strength. Mission as presence means among other things a capacity for self-exposure, about which Jacob Loewen writes so tellingly in an article bearing that title: "Self-exposure: Bridge to Fellowship." Discussing the moat that separates the foreign missionary from his national brother, and the masks that all of us wear, he presents the following outline of his thesis:

1. That just as there is a gulf between God and man, so also there are barriers, gulfs, and walls of separation between man and his fellows.

2. That all men by nature as partakers of human culture are trained to wear a variety of masks to cover their true identity.

3. That missionaries, like other men, have learned to live with masks which will stand as a barrier between them and the nationals whom they want to serve.

4. That God in the incarnation of Christ has demonstrated that man needs a "human" sympathetic priest, one who has experienced and is willing to admit the pull of temptation and the limitations of the human flesh and nature.

5. That effective witness to others, especially to people in a different culture, will require an honest differentiation between the reality of one's daily life and the ideal of one's profession.

6. That the honest facing and admission of the reality in one's life can often serve as a catalyst for a redemptive response in the life of one's brother.[6]

Dr. Loewen proceeds to illustrate his argument with several instances from his own experience and that of others in which quiet initiative taken by a missionary to admit a fault or temptation to sin had served as a catalyst for eliciting confession and restoration in some instance of strained relations or personal sin in the foreign community of which the missionary had become a part. In the opening chapter of this volume I recited in some detail a similar experience of my own.

The missionary halo is intolerable enough when worn on furlough, where the impression that anyone can be so whole or so holy turns off people struggling with their own inability to handle their imperfections. It is still more intolerable "in the field," where the addition of cultural and language barriers greatly increases the distance and the corresponding impression that the ideal a new believer may be struggling to reach is unattainable. By contrast, the frank admission of one's humanity and vulnerability can be a great encouragement to a brother in Christ, whether of one's own or another shared culture.

In the colonial era missionaries were encouraged, if not by their home boards, at least by the colonial authorities, to foster an image of invulnerability and inerrancy. I well remember my shock as a missionary novice when hearing a somewhat irritated missionary brother declare with some heat in a situation in which he had been challenged by a national: "Missionaries never lie!" It is to be hoped that they rarely do. But it is also to be hoped that when they do, they find the grace to admit it. Africa's and the world's need is for missionaries with that kind of grace.

All of us wear masks. We learn the art very early in our own culture. Urbanization and the increasing depersonalization it effects increases the tendency, for it is a convenient way to hide our insecurities when we feel lost and alone in an impersonal world. And the problem is no different for the young man or woman from the African or Amazonian or Alaskan bush who seeks his fortune in Kinshasa or Lima or Anchorage than it is for the Illinois farm youth who goes to Chicago.

Religious jargon is often employed to reinforce our masks, as anyone who ever sat through a canned testimony service knows only too well. In Westerners, as Loewen points out, masking is further reinforced by the "Western mania for privacy— privacy for dressing, privacy for talking, privacy for eating, privacy for personal belongings,"[7] including the habit of using one's native tongue when talking to fellow missionaries in the presence of nationals.

Our masks rarely serve their purpose, since the people we serve are usually astute judges of our real selves and are seldom deceived, even where supposedly well-kept secrets are concerned. And in the long run the chief deprivation is our own, for the mask shuts us off from true and redemptive fellowship with them. It also prevents us from becoming the witness for Christ which is ostensibly our motivation for being among them and sharing their lives. To unmask is to become incarnate, to relive Christ in the world.

There is a sense in which God unmasked Himself in Christ. "And the Word was made flesh and dwelt among us," John declares, "(and we beheld his glory, the glory as of the only begotten of the Father,) full of grace and truth" (John 1:14 KJV). And he invites us to follow him in such identification. "As the Father has sent me, even so send I you" (John 20:21 RSV), Jesus declared. Writes Loewen:

> If the Christ crossed the infinite-finite barrier to translate the truth of God into a form intelligible to men, Christ's disciples are sent to translate this truth across the many cultural and social barriers that separate men. If God had to become man to become intelligible to the human race, it stands to reason that finite men will have to "become men" in other cultures if their experience of God is to become intelligible in such different cultures.[8]

The Bible never depicts the man of God as perfect. Moses, Abraham, David, Peter—all the saints are presented with their failings as well as with their strengths, in spiritual defeat as well as in victory. When James suggested to his flock, "Confess your faults one to another, and pray for each other that you may be healed" (James 5:16 Phillips) he was writing for missionaries as well as others.

There is a wistful note in some recent correspondence from

a missionary committee chairman who wrote to me about a threatened split in the national church he serves, to tell of a Bible-study and prayer session that brought national pastors and missionaries together in an effort to heal the split. A sensitive spirit himself, who knows the value of self-exposure, he writes:

> Even though there were tremendous blessings as a result of intercessory prayer at home and out here, the reports given in the local regions and churches seem to have emphasized . . . divisiveness rather than the unifying force which was manifestly at work among us. *I was a little dismayed that so few missionaries took part in the "confessions" of sin which were such a major part of the work of the Spirit* [at the conference]. (Italics mine.)

Doctor Loewen continues:

> If we really want to enter into any intimate relationship with other human beings, there is a way! The way of self-exposure. We will have to be willing to be known, if we want to know. Self-exposure will be of utmost importance to the missionary, for it will reveal in real life his encounter with the values he is teaching. . . . It will prevent us from casting the first stone at the person caught in shortcoming, because we will already be kneeling at the cross in repentance for our own weaknesses.[9]

An insistence on the part of missionaries on separation, on withholding the mystery of their true selves, only contributes to the persistence of those elements in African life which foster remoteness, including the practice of magic, which remains so great a threat to the church of Africa. The missionary who understands mission as presence, and presence as self-exposure and vulnerability, helps to remove the remoteness of God, who, in the African world view, is indeed remote. To witness to the end of

this remoteness in the Incarnation of Jesus Christ while remaining remote oneself is to strengthen the hand of ancient
forces that deny God's nearness. By the same token, to be present as a person who is near in true humanity in the name of
Christ, is to reinforce the Incarnation.

Throughout the pages of Scripture we see God taking the
initiative of offering His presence to men that they may see
and know and understand that He loves them. He does so in the
garden for Adam and for Moses in the burning bush. He does
so supremely in Jesus Christ. And He has clearly chosen to continue to do so through the church, the body of Christ, the community of presence.

He has not promised that such presence will not evoke hostility. On the contrary, He suggests that hostility and persecution
are to be expected wherever the presence of the Christian community truly reflects His own designs for the world. Thus, even
where the cry "Missionary, Go Home!" is heard, it cannot be interpreted as a *prima facie* criterion for withdrawal. There is a
time and place for shaking the dust from our feet, as the New
Testament suggests (Luke 9:5). But neither the time nor the
place is best determined by rationalizations that cover for a
weariness of spirit or a loss of vision or a reaching for an alibi to
join the mad dash of our century for materialistic fullness.

Africa and the rest of the world are not rejecting friendship. What they reject is friendship that is offered on our terms,
which is not friendship at all. The world will accept missionary
presence, career or short-term, professional or self-supporting,
provided it comes as a gift of self, and not a bribe.

And suppose the gift is refused? "The disciple is not above
his Master" (Luke 6:40 KJV), declared Jesus, whose own offer
of self was rejected. There is a cross in mission. God's is a friendship pact sealed in blood. To refuse that possibility for ourselves
is to fail to understand the cross. And to refuse the cross is ultimately to disavail oneself and the world of the Resurrection.

Chapter 12

MISSION AS CROSS

We read of our Lord that "he set his face resolutely towards Jerusalem" (Luke 9:51 NEB). He knew what was awaiting Him there. There would be cheers, and there would be a cross. He had already heard the cry "Son of Man, Go Home!" and its counterpart "Son of Man, Come Back!" and He would hear more of the same. Because He never doubted that He was sent, He set his face steadfastly toward the place of encounter.

We began our discussion with the admission that the missionary is not everywhere wanted, and looked at the evidence. We moved to suggest that although this is true, it is not everywhere true and it is not the whole truth, for he is also wanted, and needed. Then we tried to suggest that the final criterion of mission is not popularity or unpopularity, need or satiety, but the fact that God sends. The initiative is His, and believing men respond to His call, and go where He sends them.

We have also taken a look at the road the disciple who hears the call and responds to the sending may walk in our age—an age of secularization, technological explosion, and resurgent nationalism. It is not an easy road to walk, more difficult perhaps than the jungle paths and rivers by which Livingstone made his way into Africa's interior in response to the same call that beckons us today. Still, we are no less impelled than he and the vast host in his train to set our face steadfastly toward the Holy City. That it looks increasingly for our times like the secular city, as urban conglomerates everywhere burgeon, and as a common world city culture emerges, does not deter us. For there live the growing masses of men, and Christ died for them.

So we have decided to accept our world, invite the new diaspora of the jet set to make tents wherever they go, and try to be all things to all men, that by all means we may save some. And lest those we seek to save should feel that in our doing so it is really our own salvation that we seek, we have wondered out loud about what presence might mean.

It wasn't our idea, of course. "Emmanuel" they called him— "God with us." The incarnation was God's act of living, participating presence in the life of man. For thirty-three years He walked among us, choking on our dust, drinking from our polluted streams, testing His immune response to the same viruses that threaten our own existence. He knew the chill of Bethlehem at birth, the gnawing hunger of the wilderness fast, the temptation to power and popularity, the betrayal of friends, an early and painful death, indeed, "the death of a common criminal" (Phil. 2:8 Phillips).

"Even so, send I you," He said (John 20:21 KJV). And there is no escaping it. Our Lord's "even so" calls for identification with men where they live, however difficult that may be, even where it means a cross.

What is identification?

It is not, of course, "going native," though we should be wrong to exclude that as a possibility. Where "going native" is interpreted largely in terms of living standards it can actually close the doors of communication, as Eugene Nida points out in *Message and Mission*. For the likely reaction of the local populace may well be: "If these Europeans know how to live better than we do, why don't they? We would if we could."[1]

I sensed something of this kind of reaction when, in the early years of our Congo experience, a single woman missionary on our staff had a native-style house built for herself in a section of the "native" village on the mission compound. It didn't really make her closer to the African than the rest of us. The important thing in missionary housing, as Stanley Soltau suggests, is not the kind of building, or the nature of the property one has, but the way one uses his facilities.[2]

But it is equally true that refusing what is native can be a barrier to communication. This is particularly true in the area of participation in meals. Refusing to eat what nationals eat is of particular importance in societies where witchcraft is still practiced, since one may thereby convey suspicion of the host, and open oneself to the suspicion of being engaged in some evil intent. Indeed, by accepting the host's food the visitor in effect puts himself under the protection of the head of the house.

I make it a practice to eat what is set before me, "asking no questions" (I Cor. 10:27 KJV). The biblical reference which this paraphrases is one passage some of my fundamentalist friends *don't* take literally!) I happen to enjoy fried termites, an African delicacy which is actually a staple when in season among the Ngbandi of the northern Congo. The fact that I enjoy it is not lost on the local populace. Our familiar proverb, "the way to a man's heart is through his stomach," may well be paraphrased, "the way to a people's heart is through your own stomach," for there are probably no cultures where the sharing of food is not a door to acceptance and communication.

It is not always easy, and there are risks. I came down with hepatitis after my most recent trip to the Congo (though I think I picked it up at a missionary's home!). On a recent visit to arctic Alaska my tolerance for the strange was taxed to the limit when I shared in eating *agutuk* with Eskimo friends. Consisting of caribou and whale fat whipped up with seal oil and served like ice cream, it very nearly pushed me over my nausea threshold. But the Eskimo ladies who served us were obviously pleased that my companion and I sampled it.

Nor does identification mean a deliberate attempt to lose one's own identity. Jesus did not surrender his Godhood in becoming man. He "was in all points tempted like as we are, yet without sin" (Hebrews 4:15 KJV). To try to become something other than oneself is to lose the very ground of true communication. True, the missionary comes with the claim of having become a new creature in Christ, but the self-denial called for in conversion is not repudiation but genuine self-discovery. It is the coming to oneself of the Prodigal who finds his way home. The call to identification is not a call to become another person. It is a call to share the self that Christ has made whole. Max Warren puts it well:

> "Identification with" does not mean loss of identity. It means the sympathetic entering into the life of another. Only by a deep mutuality can "identification with" be purged of a purely romantic and unreal significance. The missionary who leaves America or Britain for India does not go to meet his Indian colleague bearing all the burden of "identification with" on his own shoulders. Partnership involves for the Indian no less real an adventure of meeting, a no less difficult "identification with" the man from the West. The true dignity of relationship demands the recognition of mutuality.[3]

There lies the crux of identification—mutuality. Jacob Loewen devotes a paper to this reality in the July-August 1964 issue of *Practical Anthropology* under the title "Reciprocity in Identification." Mutuality or reciprocity begins with a willingness to learn—"a genuine concern for and a deep appreciation of a way of life that is different from one's own. The cheap sentimental, romantic approach, which gushes over 'native things' as if they were very quaint novelties, rather than to provide for reciprocity, will lead to psychological distance, for no one wants to be regarded lightly."[4] Nor is there a continued place for the kind of paternalism reflected in expressions like "our Africans," which are not so subtle reflections of an effort to build one's own ego, where one sees himself or his mission as the center about which orbit the people he serves.

We have suggested elsewhere that the missionary always remains a foreigner, however successfully he cuts his ties with his origins. Reciprocity in identification declares that this really doesn't matter. It is the progress made in learning, not the mastery, that matters, for continual progress spells continued caring, a witness to the respect with which one regards the culture with which he seeks communication. Smalley is doubtless right when he insists that progress in mastering a language and understanding a culture is a visible sign of true inward identification.[5] Putting the accent on progress as against mastery removes the question of natural gifts from the issue, which is of utmost importance, since people differ so widely in their learning capacities.

Learning requires humility. And a part of such humility is a self-emptying of pride which makes one willing not only to learn in order to know, but also to be known. We have discussed this at some length in the previous chapter under the subject of self-exposure, and will not do more than reiterate in this context the absolute necessity to any effort at identification of such willingness to be known. This is no small demand on Western man, who gives generously to a fault of his means and energies and knowledge, but who finds it hard to give himself.

A part of our problem is the accent in our culture on individualism, to the near exclusion of a concern for community. The overbending concern for the criminal as against the community he wrongs as expressed in recent Supreme Court decisions is one evidence of this in our own country. Another part of the problem and perhaps an extension of it is our fetishistic concern for personal privacy, to which we have already made reference. It expresses itself, as Loewen shows in some detail, in the physical closures we have developed to secure it: separate rooms for children of different sexes (indeed, often for each child); walls, fences, locks, partitions everywhere, shutting ourselves off from others while dressing (or studying, or figuring our accounts, he might have added). Where no physical walls exist, we communicate by code. For the missionary, this often means talking in his native language to other missionaries in the presence of nationals, as we pointed out above.[6]

I was recently a visitor in Hong Kong. In some of the new housing developments there, where 36,000 people may live in a single block, whole families of eight or ten people live in a single room ten by fourteen feet. In addition to living there, all of them together, with no privacy, they may also work there, using the same room for a factory employing four or five people, manufacturing some simple product or completing a single step in the making of something, the final production of which is shared by a series of such households. I wondered how long I should keep my sanity in such a situation!

Yet we shall have to learn to get along without our cherished privacy if we are to achieve identification with a world that has increasingly less and less room. The Hong Kong setting just described was characterized by an incredible din as well—noise, loud and continuous. Of this I have no fears. Our own technology is fast immunizing us to this problem. Certainly it should be no barrier for my three children of nineteen, fifteen, and eight years of age, if the stereo tapes and transistor radios to which they listen while doing their homework is any index!

Anything which shuts us off from another is a barrier to identification. Surely the fear of disease need no longer be such a barrier. I knew a missionary once who continued to boil her baby's bath water long after he crawled! Any attempt to keep ourselves thus sterile—except in the operating theater where it properly belongs—can only result in sterile efforts at communication. In the same category is a hesitancy to sleep as a stranger or guest in a proffered bed. Here again the issue is mutuality. Loewen uses the expression "exchangeability of facilities" as an example of reciprocity, and he extends the term to include not only tables and beds where one is in turn either a guest or host, but also games, which may go a long way to enhance mutual respect and acceptance. Our problem is that it is easier for us to teach volleyball than to learn to play *kisolo* (an African game played with beans on a pocketed board) or any other native game where we are bound to lose and appear awkward.

The classic New Testament passage on identification is doubtless the familiar passage in Philippians 2:5-8. I particularly like the Phillips rendition:

Let Christ himself be your example as to what your attitude should be. For he, who had always been God by nature, did not cling to his prerogatives as God's equal, but stripped himself of all privilege by consenting to be a slave by nature and being born as mortal man. And, having become man, he humbled himself by living a life of utter obedience, even to the extent of dying, AND THE DEATH HE DIED WAS THE DEATH OF A COMMON CRIMINAL. That is why God has now lifted him so high, and has given him a name beyond all names, so that at the name of Jesus "every knee shall bow," whether in Heaven or earth or under the earth. And that is why, in the end, "every tongue shall confess" that Jesus Christ is Lord, to the glory of God the Father.[7]

Mutuality is recognized at the outset in the phrase "have this mind in *yourselves*" (RSV). "Yourselves," not "yourself." Each abandons whatever privileged status he may have in favor of the other, "stripping" himself. And each accepts "the form of a servant" (RSV).

Much has been written about the servant role in mission. At the least it implies a willingness to be subordinate. It seems no accident to me that the churches with the finest record in relief work have almost universally been those which have accepted the Johannine record of Jesus' last days on earth with his disciples equally with the Synoptic Gospels, including in their liturgy the washing of each other's feet. I think, for example, of the Brethren Service Commission and the Brethren Church it represents. Without the conscious practice of servanthood it is difficult to be a servant. One wonders what the history of the church as a whole might have been if Jesus' command to "wash one another's feet" (John 13:14 KJV) had from the start and throughout church history been taken as seriously as the command to remember him in the breaking of the bread and the sharing of the cup expressed in Holy Communion. We may well have been more humble!

"Servant" in Scripture implies not simply subservience, but actual service. Obedience to God is an existential thing, a constant hearing and response to what is heard. And the Bible makes it abundantly clear that obedience to God is expressed in service to our fellow men.

Such service brings self-fulfillment, but it must not be motivated by the desire for such. Paul makes that clear in his insistence on self-emptying. There is a danger in any call which suggests: "Be a missionary, and fulfill yourself." The call to mission is not a call to escape. It is a call to share, to know and be known, to listen and be heard, to find together the will of God for ourselves and those we serve.

Dr. Kenneth Cragg, in *The Call of the Minaret*,[8] tries to say what this means in the world of Islam. To identify with Islam means for the Christian a costly experience in genuine dialogue, a seeking to enter into the will of God for the Muslim. Robert Lee attempts something of the same in a study of Christian mission in Japan, appropriately entitling his book *Stranger in the Land*.[9] Both seem to suggest that identification with a people in our time means investing our lives in the service of the problems they face, for "the meaning of Christian compassion is that problems become persons, and cases people."[10]

Certainly compassion is the Christ's own motivation. "He had compassion on them," or him, or her, is an oft-recurring phrase in the Gospels. "Compassion" may be a better word than that much abused four-letter word "love," for it conveys the note of mutuality and reciprocity of which we have been writing. It is far from pity, for it goes out and not down, knowing that the bearer shares with his fellow human being a common sinfulness and a common grace, the first a fact of their common humanity, the second a fact of God's concern for them both, expressed at its highest in Christ's redemptive act on the Cross.

Ultimately, any effort at identification must accept the possibility that following Jesus on the road to Jerusalem may well mean climbing the hill of Golgotha. The church at its best has always known this. And there have been reminders in our own time that identification in life may have to mean identification in death. Dr. Clarence A. Nelson captures the truth of this in these lines:

> Whatever of good or bad can be said about the church of Christ, it is historically true that it has always had some people who have understood and obeyed the voice of their Lord. From the blood of Stephen, the church's first martyr, until today, there has been a multitude that has not counted

its life dear that it might finish its course. They have known they were expendable, and yet they have been of all people most indispensable. They took their commission from Christ seriously and witnessed the good evidence to a generation not wanting what it needed most.[11]

He was writing about Dr. Paul Carlson, my successor at the Wasolo hospital in the northern Congo, who accepted his expendability, indispensable as he was to a hundred thousand people for whom he was the only physician. Paul had prepared for his career by studying anthropology as well as medicine. He wanted to understand people as well as serve them. Wanting to understand is as important as wanting to serve, and the first step in knowing and being known. So motivated, he found it easier than most to accept the facts of the new situation in which missionaries had to work in post-independence Congo. In the hospital at Wasolo, this meant accepting as administrator a Congolese nurse-aide with only five years of primary school, two years of nurse's training, and some years of experience in mission hospitals and clinics. Sebastian Wanzi and Paul Carlson became true friends who mutually respected each other.

It also meant accepting the Cross, not as an isolated single fact of human history, but as a possibility for himself as a follower of Jesus Christ. Thus he died in a hail of bullets triggered by a nervous finger at the very moment of rescue as a prisoner in Stanleyville. In this Paul Carlson took Christ as his example. "He did not cling to his prerogatives" as a Western man. Educated in anthropology, trained as a physician and surgeon, certified in tropical medicine and the French language—"he stripped himself" of the privileges which his cultural and educational background qualified him to exercise, and became a servant of the Congolese people. He served them unstintingly, and when taken by the rebels, he remembered Jesus' command not to return evil for evil, but to "do good to those who hate you" (Luke 6:27 RSV), and he fed them and gave them drink and treated their wounds.

The Congolese themselves recognized this. When he was buried at the small cemetery in Karawa (where black and white now lie side by side) there was a moment of tension between the Congolese military guard sent to honor him and the leaders of the Church of Christ in the Ubangi as to who should bear the casket! Shortly after his death I received a letter from Zacharie Alenge, president of the church, saying in part:

> Truly we have great sorrow because of the death of our brother because we know his humility, kindness, and desire to help us Congolese. . . . Although his desire was only to help us, the people of Congo, yet he was killed here.[12]

Enoc Sakofio, director of primary schools, speaking at the burial service, added:

> He has died in our hands and it gives us much sorrow. . . . Paul died for his people. As Jesus said in John 10:11—"I will die for my sheep," so Paul died for us.[13]

Paul Carlson was "obedient even unto death." In this, he accepted complete identity with the people he came to serve, a fact they recognized. The identity in death was symbolized by two of the hospital staff, Ambroise Kokembe, and Boniface Bomba, whom the rebels killed when Paul was taken prisoner. To the Congolese it was significant that Paul left his bones among them, and in the midst of sorrow they were glad. Sakofio put it well to the missionaries and others gathered at the grave:

> In French they talk about "*perte*." We have indeed sustained a great loss. Paul is lost to us. . . . Today he is dead,

and as we think of it we have great sorrow. We are glad, however, that his body has been brought to us to be buried among his brothers. . . . Send a letter to his mother and father and his relatives that we are glad they agreed that he be buried among us. When we go by, we will see his grave because he agreed to die among us. He didn't want to leave us, and for that those who killed him did not kill him, but us.

We do not know English to write to them so you are our *"porte parole,"* or messenger, to bear our message to them. It is as though we should write to them that when we saw Paul's casket, we were happy. We prayed and prayed for Paul, with sorrow, with weariness. People sat by their radios and listened to hear if Paul had been released, or what should happen to Paul. We prayed much. But God's will was done, not the will of man. Let us thank God for what He has done. In the name of Christ Jesus. Amen.[14]

There is a sense in which every martyr helps to complete "what is lacking in Christ's afflictions for the sake of his body, that is, the church" (Col. 1:24 RSV). The Apostle Paul does not suggest in these lines that Jesus' sacrifice was in any sense incomplete or insufficient for man's salvation. He is simply saying that Christ's servanthood and suffering must be relived in each generation for the sins of men if the cross on which He was lifted up is truly to draw all men unto Himself. While the Congo event was still fresh, these lines were written:

The civilized world was horrified at the waste and sense-less brutality of the Stanleyville massacre. Yet there is an element of poetic justice in all of this—if we can say it without being misunderstood. If it seems inordinately cruel to us that the nobly innocent should be among those to bear retribution in their bodies for the past sins of their race, simply recall that this is the way God works when he involves himself in redemptive activity for men . . . there is a sense in which Paul Carlson was the victim of God's inscrutable justice. God visits "the iniquity of the fathers upon the children to the third and fourth generation" (Exod. 20:5). Africa's cup of vengeance is spilling over from the awakened memory of the ignominious slave trade in which the fathers of our race indulged for too long. And we have not seen the last victim. "Though the mills of God grind slowly, yet they grind exceeding small."[15]

It may be added that Dr. Carlson's death lifted the onus of two evacuations during times of trouble from the shoulders of missionaries of the Evangelical Mission of the Ubangi. The majority of the people in the Ubangi certainly did not interpret the evacuation of missionaries in 1960 and again in 1964 as most of the folks at home did. In this they were joined by many of the missionaries themselves, some of whom are still scarred by the experience of having to abandon their place of service under the duress of majority rule and orders from the home board. The Congolese were hard put to understand why those who had come to tell them about the power and love of God should find Him inadequate to their personal needs when they were threatened. "Where is their peace?" they asked me at Wasolo in 1960, and they quoted from John 10 (paraphrased): "The hireling flees, but the Good Shepherd abides with the sheep." With Paul's and Kokembe's and Bomba's death they understood the missionaries better. The very real problem of how a husbandless wife would rear the children God had given her and her husband struck home. They were at last willing to believe that a part of the missionaries' motivation in evacuation had been to spare *them*—the Congolese—from too close identification with an agency of foreign origin so that the leaders of the church might survive to give it strength and direction in the difficult days that lay ahead.

A gospel which excludes the cross is not the Gospel of our Lord Jesus Christ. It certainly is not a gospel that can win today's world. Our Lord does not ask us to *seek* martyrdom. Ultimately, that is simply a high form of self-seeking. He does ask us to be willing to follow Him to the death, identifying with a needy and sinful world that it may know His love.

The Apostle Paul understood this well, and he described himself as a slave of Christ. I understood it in a small way myself in an existential moment in the Congo in August 1960, when the Risen Christ was very near, and I doubt that any other words I might now try to frame could express it better than the free verse to which that moment gave birth.

PRISONER

I am a prisoner.
From within the walls that hold me
Let me cry out;
I am a prisoner of Congo
And I cannot escape!

"Stone walls do not a prison make"
Was truly writ for me,
For I am held by human need, and not by stone.
I am not mortar bound, but mortal tied.
My prison is vast, and I am free
To roam rough roads and jungle trails at will.
I do not lack for light of sun,
Nor sight of stars, nor kiss of breeze . . .
Yet I am imprisoned truly.

I am prisoner of a woman who
Six times has felt the pain of childbirth
And never once its joy. This time
She counts on me to hear a baby's cry.

I am encircled by a band of children—
Hot-bodied babes, malnourished tots,

Worm-sluggish students—
To each of whom I bring a hope for health.

I am the captive of a devoted Sister
Smiling her Madonna-like smile through white hood,
Risking brutal theft of the chastity she offers Christ
To minister to those who hate her race.

And I am held by Him who came proclaiming
Release to all the captives of the earth.
I am a prisoner of Christ in Congo—
And I would not escape.

His slave or His prisoner. Does it really matter? Congo or
Colombia or Chicago. Does that matter either? For to be His
slave, to be His prisoner, is to be truly free. And to share His
freedom become yours with fellow human beings is the essence
of Mission.

Notes

CHAPTER 1

1. Vachel Lindsay, "The Congo," from *Collected Poems of Vachel Lindsay* (New York, The Macmillan Company, 1914, 1942).

2. Quoted by 'Nicodemus', *Renascence* (Faber 1943, p. 60). From John V. Taylor, *The Primal Vision* (Philadelphia, Fortress Press, 1963), p. 202.

3. The material in this chapter, as well as parts of Chapters 2 and 5, is adapted from an article which appeared originally in *The Covenant Quarterly*, February 1964, under the title "Reflections on a Legacy"; and which subsequently appeared, slightly adapted, in *World Vision Magazine*, May 1967, retitled "Whitey, Your Time Is Running Out." Under the latter title it has also been reprinted by *Practical Anthropology*, September-October 1968, and *Freedom Now*, Vol. 4, No. 2 (March-April 1968).

CHAPTER 2

1. D. Rinchon, *La traite et l'esclavage des Congolais par les Européans* (Bruxelles, 1929), p. 133. Elmer Neufeld, *The Unfinished Revolution*, Report of the Mennonite Central Committee, Akron, Pa., Vol. 6. No. 1 (Spring 1963), p. 9. I am much indebted to this fine paper.

2. Pierre Ryckmans, *Dominer pour servir* (Nouvelle Edition; Bruxelles, L'Edition Universelle, 1948).

3. Laurens van der Post, *The Dark Eye in Africa* (New York, William Morrow and Company, Inc., 1955), pp. 116–117.

4. Alan P. Merriam, *Congo, Background of Conflict* (Chicago, Northwestern University Press, 1961), p. 36.

5. John and Rena Karefa-Smart, *The Halting Kingdom: Christianity and the African Revolution*, quoted by Ralph E. Dodge, *The Unpopular Missionary* (Westwood, N.J., Fleming H. Revell Company, 1964), p. 39.

6. Dodge, *loc. cit.*

7. Arden Almquist, *Covenant Missions in Alaska* (Chicago, Covenant Press, 1962), p. 151.

8. *Ibid.*

9. Lesslie Newbigin, *Trinitarian Faith and Today's Mission* (Richmond, Va., John Knox Press, 1964), p. 68.

10. Colin M. Turnbull, *The Lonely African* (Anchor Books Edition; Garden City, N.Y., Doubleday and Company, Inc., 1963), p. 9.

11. *Ibid.*, pp. 16–17.

12. Alan Paton, *Cry, The Beloved Country* (Oxford, The Alden Press, 1948), p. 252.

13. Titus M. Johnson, *When Congo Burst Its Seams* (Minneapolis, Minn., Free Church Press, 1961).

CHAPTER 3

1. William J. Lederer and Eugene Burdick, *The Ugly American* (New York, W. W. Norton and Company, Inc., 1958).

2. Ralph E. Dodge, *The Unpopular Missionary* (Westwood, N.J., Fleming H. Revell Company, 1964).

3. James Scherer, *Missionary, Go Home!* (Englewood Cliffs, N.J., Prentice-Hall, Inc., 1964).

4. *Christian Times*, July 7, 1968, p. 4.

5. *Christian Century*, December 13, 1967, p. 1605.

6. Ronan Hoffman, as reported by *Christianity Today*, October 13, 1967, p. 43.

7. Frederick Dale Bruner, "The American Missionary Problem—An Essay in Conscience," *Christian Century*, June 5, 1968, p. 751. Copyright © 1968, Christian Century Foundation. Reprinted by permission.

8. *Ibid.*

9. *Ibid.*

10. *Ibid.*

11. *Ibid.*

12. *Ibid.*, p. 752.

13. *Ibid.*, p. 753.

14. *La Jolla Presbyterian,* November 30, 1967, p. 3.

15. Barnerd M. Luben, Radio, Visual Education and Mass Communication Committee of the National Council of Churches. From a news release by John Mullen, National Council of Churches, New York, N.Y., May 3, 1968.

CHAPTER 4

1. William J. Petersen, *Another Hand on Mine* (New York, McGraw-Hill, 1967), p. 13.

2. Delbert A. Kuehl, *Christianity Today,* November 10, 1967, p. 149.

3. *Christian Times,* May 12, 1968, p. 6.

4. Hugh Steven, *Christian Times,* August 18, 1968, p. 6.

5. See, e.g., *Moody Monthly,* June 1968; *World Vision Magazine,* April 1968.

6. *Christianity Today,* October 13, 1967, p. 43.

7. *Ibid.*

8. Nene Ramientos, "Should Missionaries Get Out of the Philippines?" *World Vision Magazine,* November 1968, p. 21.

9. *Ibid.,* p. 22.

10. *Ibid.*

11. *Ibid.*

12. *Ibid.*

13. I use the term "younger churches" to describe the churches born of the missionary movement of the past century, simply because no better term is available. To describe something as "younger" in today's world no longer carries the inference that it is therefore inferior. Indeed, the contrary is fast becoming true! I am merely using a chronological category as a means of distinguishing them from the churches of the West, to whom this volume mainly addresses itself.

14. See also, e.g., *World Vision Magazine,* April 1968, p. 22ff.

15. See also Douglas Webster, *Yes to Mission* (New York, Seabury Press, 1966). His candid appraisal of the strengths and weaknesses of the "younger churches" as well as the positive note suggested in both the title and the volume itself make it a most valuable book.

CHAPTER 5

1. L. H. Gann and Peter Duignan, *Burden of Empire* (Hoover Institution Publication; New York, Frederick A. Praeger, 1967), p. 382.

2. *Ibid.,* p. 360.

3. *Ibid.*, p. 362.

4. *Ibid.*, p. 363.

5. *Ibid.*

6. *Ibid.*, p. 365.

7. *Ibid.*, p. 367.

8. *Ibid.*, pp. 368–369.

9. Lord Hailey, *An African Survey: A Study of Problems Arising in Africa South of the Sahara* (rev. ed., London, 1957), p. 1298. From Gann and Duignan, *op. cit.*, p. 369 n.

10. George Martelli, *Leopold to Lumumba: A History of the Belgian Congo, 1877–1960* (London, 1962), pp. 215–216. From Gann and Duignan, *op. cit.*, p. 369.

11. Gann and Duignan, *loc. cit.*

12. *Ibid.*, p. 371.

13. It should be pointed out that Portuguese oppression in Angola in recent years has driven thousands (though not millions) of refugees into the Congo. But it is equally true that in independent Sudan *Africans* have forced equal numbers of other Africans from that country.

14. See *Africa Now*, No. 45 (July-August 1969), p. 3.

15. See Arend Th. van Leeuwen, *Christianity in World History* (London, Edinburgh House Press, 1964), pp. 411–422. This is the definitive volume in any discussion of secularization, particularly in reference to its impact on the Third World.

16. Lesslie Newbigin, *Trinitarian Faith and Today's Mission* (Richmond, Va., John Knox Press, 1964), p. 52.

17. *Ibid.*, p. 53.

18. Wesley Nelson, *Salvation and Secularity* (Chicago, Covenant Press, 1969), p. 19.

CHAPTER 6

1. Arthur Glasser, "Current Strategy in Missions," *His* magazine reprint, n.d., p. 10.

2. Dave Christensen, "Tell It Like It Is, Dave," *Africa Now*, June 1968, p. 3.

3. Eugene Smith, *God's Mission and Ours* (New York, Abingdon Press, 1961), p. 59. My use of Dr. Smith's lines in this context should not be interpreted as identifying him with the universalist position.

4. Harold Lindsell, "Missionary Imperatives: A Conservative Evangelical Exposition," in *Protestant Crosscurrents in Mission*, ed. Norman A. Horner (Nashville and New York, Abingdon Press, 1968), p. 58. Reprinted by permission.

5. David Stowe, "Foreign Missions Today—A Spent Force?," *Tempo*, December 15, 1968, p. 4.

6. Richard Shaull, "Toward A Reformation of Objectives," *Protestant Crosscurrents in Mission* (Nashville and New York, Abingdon Press, 1968), p. 90.

7. Kenneth Strachan, "Call To Witness," *International Review of Missions*, April 1964, p. 211.

8. Shaull, *op. cit.*, p. 93.

9. *Ibid.*, p. 94.

CHAPTER 7

1. Philip Zabriskie, *That Which God Has Cleansed* (lecture given at the Nineteenth Ecumenical Student Conference on the Christian World Mission, Ohio University, Athens, Ohio) (New York, National Student Christian Federation, 1964). Mr. Zabriskie's imaginative exposition of Acts 10 is a most helpful attempt to place the issue of secularization in a relevant biblical context.

2. *Ibid.*, pp. 4–5.

3. *Ibid.*, p. 6.

4. Thomas E. Clarke, "Collegiality, Mission, and Laity," in *Revolution in Missionary Thinking*, ed. William J. Richardson (Maryknoll, N.Y., Maryknoll Publications, 1966), p. 185.

5. Noted by Lesslie Newbigin, "The Healing Ministry in the Mission of the Church," *The Healing Church; The Tübingen Consultation*, 1964 (World Council of Churches, Geneva, 1965), p. 9.

6. Robert C. Mitchell, "Healing in the Church of the Lord Aladura," *African Attitudes to Health and Healing* (collection of papers from the library of the Christian Medical Council, New York) p. 7.

7. T. A. Lambo, "Problems of Adjustment Between Traditional Medicine and Modern Methods of Medical Practice," *ibid.*, pp. 1–2.

8. Robert C. Mitchell, "Witchcraft, Sin, Divine Power and Healing: The Aladura Churches and the Attainment of Life's Destiny Among the Yoruba," *ibid.*, p. 13.

9. Michael Gelfand, *Medicine and Custom in Africa* (Edinburgh and London, E. and S. Livingstone, Ltd., 1964), p. 47.

10. See for example, the poem "Les Vautours," by the Haitian poet David Diop obtainable in French from *Coups de pilon* (Paris, 1960), p. 8; translated by Ulli Beier in J. Langston Hughes, ed., *Poems from Black Africa* (Bloomington, Ind. Bloomcraft Press, 1963), p. 145.

11. J. Merle Davis, *New Buildings on Old Foundations* (New York and London, International Missionary Council, 1947), p. 233.

12. Arend Th. van Leeuwen, *Christianity in World History* (London, Edinburgh House Press, 1964), p. 429.

13. John Wilkinson, "Christian Healing and the Congregation," *The Healing Church* (cited above), p. 32.

14. Mitchell, "Witchcraft, Sin, Divine Power and Healing" (cited above), p. 12.

15. Quoted by Eliot Elisofon, "African Sculpture," *Atlantic*, Vol. 203, No. 4 (April 1959), 49.

16. Eugene A. Nida and William A. Smalley, *Introducing Animism* (New York, Friendship Press, 1959), p. 50.

17. Mitchell, "Healing in the Church of the Lord Aladura" (cited above), p. 40.

18. Paul Tournier, *A Doctor's Casebook* (Westchester, N.Y., Good News Publishers, 1958), pp. 20–21. Condensed from the book of the same title (London, SCM Press, Ltd., 1960), translated from the French by Edwin Hudson.

19. Gelfand, *op. cit.*, p. 63.

20. Erling Kayser, "Medicine and Modern Philosophy: An Introduction." *The Healing Church, op. cit.*, pp. 22–23. I am also indebted to Martin Scheel for his excellent paper in the same volume (pp. 24–28) entitled "Some Comments on Pre-Scientific Forms of Healing."

21. *The Healing Church, op. cit.*, p. 35.

22. Much of this chapter and part of Chapter Six are adapted from a paper first presented at the University of Kansas Post-Graduate Seminar on Medicine and Religion, Kansas City, Kansas, October 25–26, 1966, under the title "The Physician Looks at Religion in the Care of the Sick: The Medical Missionary," and subsequently published as an *Occasional Bulletin* from the Missionary Research Library, New York, April, 1967, Vol. 28, No. 4 (April 1967), retitled "Medicine and Religion—A Missionary Perspective." Under the latter title it also appeared as a reprint in *Practical Anthropology*, Vol. 15, No. 5 (September-October 1968).

CHAPTER 8

1. Hendrik Kraemer. *World Cultures and World Religions—The Coming Dialogue*, p. 353. Published in the U.S.A. 1960, The Westminster Press. Copyright © 1960, Hendrik Kraemer. Used by permission.

2. *Ibid.*, p. 355.

3. *Ibid.*, p. 356.

4. *Ibid.*, p. 364 n.

5. *Ibid.*, p. 365.

6. *Ibid.*, p. 366.

7. Eugene Nida, *Religion Across Cultures* (New York, Evanston, and London, Harper and Row, 1968), pp. 60–62.

8. *Ibid.*, p. 66.

9. Eric Fife and Arthur Glasser, *Missions In Crisis* (Chicago, Inter-Varsity Press, 1961), p. 168.

10. Paul S. Rees, "Christian Infiltrators," *World Vision Magazine,* February 1968, p. 47.

11. Steven G. Mackie, "The Tent-Making Ministry," *World Mission Newsletter,* Vol. 14, No. 2 (May 1967), p. 1.

12. *Ibid.*

13. Ralph Winter, ed. *Theological Education by Extension* (South Pasadena, Calif., William Carey Library, 1969).

14. R. Park Johnson, *Religion in Shoes—The Churchman Overseas and Christian Opportunity,* (pamphlet; New York, The Committee on American Laymen Overseas, National Council of Churches, n.d.), p. 1.

15. *Ibid.*, p. 2.

16. *Ibid.*, p. 4.

17. R. B. Kochtitsky, "LAOS—Laymen's Overseas Service," *Occasional Bulletin* (New York, Missionary Research Library), Vol. 16, No. 11 (November 1965), p. 2.

18. *Ibid.*, p. 2.

19. *Ibid.*, p. 3.

20. Fife and Glasser, *op. cit.*, p. 163.

CHAPTER 9

1. Robert Lee, *Stranger in the Land* (New York, Friendship Press, 1967).

2. D. T. Niles, *Upon the Earth* (New York, McGraw-Hill, 1962), p. 34.

3. Jacob A. Loewen, "The Church: Indigenous and Ecumenical," *Practical Anthropology* (P.O. Box 307, Tarrytown, N.Y. 10591), Vol. 11, No. 6 (November-December 1964), p. 246.

4. Russell A. Cervin, "Nes Ammim", *Covenant Companion,* March 20, 1964, p. 5.

5. *Ibid.*

6. Roy E. Shearer, "Jesus Abbey: Monastery for Moderns," *World Vision Magazine,* November 1968, pp. 10–13.

7. John A. Bell, "Individual and Group Responsibility for the Needy Churches," in *Revolution in Missionary Thinking*, ed. William J. Richardson (Maryknoll, N.Y., Maryknoll Publications, 1966), pp. 47–48.

8. Michael Kelly, "Commentary from Abroad," *ibid.*, p. 16; J. Gerard Grondin, "Cooperation: Key to Apostolic Action," *ibid.*, p. 73.

CHAPTER 10

1. D. T. Niles, *Upon the Earth* (New York, McGraw-Hill, 1962), p. 38.

CHAPTER 11

1. John V. Taylor, *The Primal Vision* (Philadelphia, Fortress Press, 1964), p. 17.

2. William J. Samarin, "Language of Silence," *Practical Anthropology* (P.O. Box 307, Tarrytown, N.Y. 10591), Vol. 12, No. 3 (May-June 1965), p. 118.

3. Ralph Harper, *The Sleeping Beauty* (London, Harvill Press, 1956), p. 111.

4. Taylor, *op. cit.*, p. 196.

5. *Ibid.*, pp. 196–197.

6. Jacob A. Loewen, "Self-Exposure: Bridge to Fellowship," *Practical Anthropology* (P.O. Box 307, Tarrytown, N.Y. 10591), Vol. 12, No. 2 (March-April 1965), p. 50.

7. *Ibid.*, p. 54.

8. *Ibid.*, p. 55.

9. *Ibid.*, p. 56.

CHAPTER 12

1. Eugene A. Nida, *Message and Mission* (New York, Harper and Brothers, 1960), p. 162.

2. Stanley Soltau, *Missions at Crossroads* (Grand Rapids, Mich., Baker Book House, 1954), p. 118.

3. Max Warren, "The Meaning of Identification," in Gerald Anderson, ed., *The Theology of the Christian Mission* (New York, McGraw-Hill, 1961), p. 232.

4. Jacob A. Loewen, "Reciprocity in Identification," *Practical Anthropology*, Vol. 11, No. 4 (July-August 1964), p. 148.

5. William A. Smalley, "Editorial Remarks: Respect and Ethnocentrism," *Practical Anthropology*, Vol. 5, No. 4 (January-February 1958), p. 191.

6. Loewen, *op. cit.*, p. 151.

7. J. B. Phillips, *The New Testament in Modern English* (New York, Macmillan Company, 1958), p. 423, Philippians 2:5–8. Used by permission.

8. Kenneth Cragg, *The Call of the Minaret* (New York, Oxford University Press, 1956).

9. Robert Lee, *Stranger in the Land* (New York, Friendship Press, 1967).

10. Cragg, *op. cit.*, p. 214.

11. Clarence A. Nelson, "Paul Carlson, Witness," in Carl Philip Anderson, *There Was a Man* (Chicago, Covenant Press, 1965), p. 87.

12. Arden Almquist, "Paul Carlson, Martyr," *ibid.*, p. 96.

13. *Ibid.*, p. 107.

14. *Ibid.*, p. 105.

15. *Ibid.*, p. 101.